FORTRESS • 45

# GERMAN DEFENCES IN ITALY IN WORLD WAR II

**NEIL SHORT**

ILLUSTRATED BY CHRIS TAYLOR

*Series editors* Marcus Cowper and Nikolai Bogdanovic

First published in Great Britain in 2006 by Osprey Publishing,
Midland House, West Way, Botley, Oxford OX2 0PH, UK
44-02 23rd St, Suite 219, Long Island City, NY 11101, USA
Email: info@ospreypublishing.com

Transferred to digital print on demand 2010

First published 2006
1st impression 2006

Printed and bound by Cadmus Communications, USA

A CIP catalogue record for this book is available from the British Library

ISBN: 978 1 84176 938 7

Design by Ken Vail Graphic Design, Cambridge, UK
Cartography by The Map Studio Ltd, Romsey, UK
Index by Alison Worthington
Originated by United Graphics, Singapore
Typeset in Monotype Gill Sans and ITC Stone Serif

**Dedication**
This book is dedicated to the memory of the men of all nationalities who fought and died in Italy.

**Acknowledgements**
The author would like to thank the many people who helped in the production of this title. In particular I would like to thank
Daniele Guglielmi, Bernard Lowry, Jeff Plowman and Gordon Rottman. As ever special thanks also go to my wife and daughter
and the rest of my family.

**Imperial War Museum collections**
Many of the photos in this book come from the Imperial War Museum's huge collections, which cover all aspects of conflict
involving Britain and the Commonwealth since the start of the 20th century. These rich resources are available online to search,
browse and buy at www.iwmcollections.org.uk. In addition to Collections Online, you can visit the Visitor Rooms where you can
explore over 8 million photographs, thousands of hours of moving images, the largest sound archive of its kind in the world,
thousands of diaries and letters written by people in wartime, and a huge reference library. To make an appointment,
call (020) 7416 5320, or e-mail mail@iwm.org.uk. Imperial War Museum www.iwm.org.uk

**The Fortress Study Group (FSG)**
The object of the FSG is to advance the education of the public in the study of all aspects of fortifications and their armaments,
especially works constructed to mount or resist artillery. The FSG holds an annual conference in September over a long weekend
with visits and evening lectures, an annual tour abroad lasting about eight days, and an annual Members' Day. The FSG journal
FORT is published annually, and its newsletter Casemate is published three times a year. Membership is international.
For further details, please contact: The Secretary, c/o 6 Lanark Place, London, W9 1BS, UK. Website: www.fsgfort.com

**The Woodland Trust**
Osprey Publishing is supporting the Woodland Trust, the UK's leading woodland conservation charity, by funding
the dedication of trees.

**www.ospreypublishing.com**

# Contents

# Introduction

In August 1943 the President of the United States, the British Prime Minister and the Combined Chiefs-of-Staff met at Casablanca to formulate future Allied strategy. The decisions they took at this meeting related to the whole conduct of the war against the Axis in Europe, but were particularly relevant to the strategy in the Mediterranean. The main aims were to eliminate Italy as a belligerent and to maintain the pressure on German forces to create the conditions for Operation *Overlord* and the eventual landings in southern France.

By this time Mussolini had been overthrown and, soon afterwards, an armistice was signed with Italy, which only left the final aim of maintaining pressure on German forces. Different people interpreted this in different ways. Certainly Churchill believed Italy offered an inviting avenue of attack against what he saw as the 'soft underbelly'[1] of the Third Reich. And following the Allied landings on the Italian mainland he hoped that Field Marshal Alexander's Fifteenth Army Group would make a rapid advance up the peninsula. However, geography, history and a resourceful enemy meant that the chances of realizing the Prime Minister's aspirations were slim.

For someone like Churchill with such a sharp military mind it should have been apparent that the topography of Italy favoured defence. 'The mountains are rugged and the Apennines make a continuous barrier between the eastern and western sides of the country. Many rivers, some fast flowing between precipitous banks, lie across the path of forces advancing from the south.'[2] To make matters worse the weather in Italy is often inclement. The summers are very hot, especially in the south, the winters are cold and the spring and autumn are often wet, which gives an attacking army only a short window for operations.

Churchill was also well versed in military history and should have known that in the long history of what is now modern Italy, few armies have enjoyed success. The Gauls sacked Rome in 390 BC and, more famously, Hannibal crossed the Alps with his elephants and defeated a superior Roman army at Cannae in 216 BC, but even he was unable to capture the Eternal City. A little over 600 years later, in AD 410, as the Roman Empire collapsed, Rome was again sacked, this time by barbarians who crossed the Alps before seizing the city.

The barbarians, or Goths, retained their grip on the peninsula for some time, but the Eastern Romans, or Byzantines, under Emperor Justinian were determined to restore as much of the Western Roman Empire as possible and, in AD 535, the Emperor ordered Belisarius, one of his young, gifted commanders, to attack. He quickly captured Sicily and then crossed to the mainland where, after a bitter struggle, he captured Naples before advancing on Rome, which fell to his army in AD 536 without a fight. The following year Belisarius successfully defended Rome against the Goths and then advanced north to take Mediolanum (Milan) and the Goth's capital of Ravenna in AD 540.

This was the first and only time that Rome has been captured from the south[3] and gave some idea of the challenge that faced Field Marshal Alexander in spite of the fact that he commanded a modern mechanized army supported by the Desert Air Force (DAF). Not only did Alexander have to cope with

---

[1] W. Churchill, *The Hinge of Fate, Vol. IV, The Second World War* (Cassell: London, 1951), p.433.
[2] C. Molony, *The Mediterranean and Middle East, Vol. V, The Campaign in Sicily and the Campaign in Italy, 3rd September to 31st March 1944* (HMSO: London, 1973), p192.
[3] The Italian patriot and soldier of fortune Giuseppe Garibaldi invaded Sicily with his 'Thousand Red Shirts' in 1860 and then crossed to the mainland where he captured Naples and advanced on Rome in 1862, but he was not able to capture the city, although Rome was eventually absorbed into the new Italian state in 1870.

difficult country and climate and achieve what had only been accomplished once in over 1,000 years, he also faced a stubborn enemy.

After the loss of Sicily the Germans had originally anticipated falling back to the Apennines, but Kesselring, the commander of Army Group C, convinced Hitler of the merit of a stand further south. This would keep the Allies further from Germany; stop them creating air bases in Italy capable of attacking industrial targets in southern Germany or, more importantly, the Ploesti oil fields in Romania; and would also ensure that the symbolically important city of Rome would not be captured. German forces were rushed south and, having failed to repulse the Allied invasion, they fought a dogged rearguard action. This provided time for engineers, construction workers and labourers to build a series of defensive lines that took advantage of the country's many rivers and mountains. These were established from the ankle of the boot to its very top and were so numerous that the Germans used almost every letter in the military phonetic alphabet. Indeed in some respects the naming of the various lines seems to have been more taxing for the Germans than it was to construct them. They included letters of the alphabet; names of both sexes from Albert to Viktor and Barbara to Paula; almost all the colours of the rainbow; historical figures from Caesar to Genghis Khan; and, less adventurously, local place names. One line was even named after the Führer himself (although this was soon changed so as to avoid the Allies gaining a major propaganda coup).

In the end more than 40 defensive lines were established, but a lack of manpower and raw materials meant that the defences were too few in number, they lacked depth and were often poorly constructed. Yet in spite of this the fortifications did serve to delay the Allies. From the initial landings in September 1943 they took the best part of two years to reach the Alps; this was no soft underbelly but was in fact a 'tough old gut'.

# Chronology

| 1922 | October | Mussolini becomes Prime Minister |
|------|---------|----------------------------------|
| 1925 | January | Mussolini announces dictatorship |
| 1935 | 3 October | Italy invades Abyssinia |
| 1936 | 9 May | Italy annexes Abyssinia |
| 1939 | 7 April | Italy invades Albania |
| 1940 | 10 June | Italy declares war on Britain and France |
| | 21 June | Italy attacks France |
| | 12 September | Italy invades Egypt from Libya |
| | 21 September | Italy signs Tripartite Pact |
| | 28 October | Italy invades Greece |
| 1941 | 11 February | Rommel arrives in North Africa after Italian reverses |
| | 11 December | Italy declares war on the USA |
| 1942 | 1 July | First battle of El Alamein |
| | 24 October | Second Battle of El Alamein |
| | 8 November | Operation *Torch* landings in North Africa |
| 1943 | 13 May | Axis forces capitulate in North Africa |
| | 10 July | Allies land in Sicily |
| | 25 July | Mussolini resigns and is arrested |
| | 17 August | Axis resistance ends in Sicily |
| | 3 September | Allies land on Italian mainland |
| | 8 September | Italy surrenders |
| | 9 September | Allies land at Salerno |
| | 10 September | Germans occupy northern Italy |
| 1944 | 27 January | Allies land at Anzio |
| | 1 February | First battle of Monte Cassino |
| | 14 February | Second battle of Monte Cassino |
| | 15 March | Third battle of Monte Cassino |
| | 11 May | Fourth battle of Monte Cassino. Monastery is captured and Allies breach Hitler Line |
| | 4 June | US troops enter Rome |
| | 4 August | Allies enter Florence |
| | 25 August | Attack on Gothic Line begins |
| 1945 | 21 April | Allies capture Bologna |
| | 28 April | Mussolini shot by partisans |
| | 29 April | Germans sign surrender terms for their troops in Italy to take effect on 2 May |

# Design and development

By the beginning of 1943 the face of the war had changed dramatically for Germany and the other Axis powers. On every front and in every field of combat the Wehrmacht was now on the defensive. In the oceans the U-boats had turned from hunter to hunted, in the air the Luftwaffe had to contend with Allied bombing raids on Germany and on land the army had been defeated at Stalingrad and was on the retreat in North Africa.

Yet in spite of this reversal of fortune, Hitler was determined not to yield any territory to the Allies. This desire, bordering on an obsession, manifested itself in his insistence that 'the southern periphery of Europe, whose bastions were the Balkans and the larger Italian islands, must be held.'[4] However, this resolve was complicated by uncertainty over what the Allies' strategy would be in the Mediterranean. Hitler was of the opinion that Sardinia was the most obvious target for an invasion, while others in the Oberkommando der Wehrmacht (OKW) believed they would attack Sicily. And these divisions were exacerbated by Operation *Mincemeat*, a clever deception plan conceived by the Allies to convince the Germans that the next attack would be directed towards the Balkans. To make matters worse Hitler, in theory at least, was still part of an Axis with Fascist Italy and Mussolini was keen to continue the fight alongside his more powerful ally.

In spite of all this uncertainty one thing was clear. The threat of invasion could not be ignored and steps would need to be taken to protect the exposed coastline. However, with the time and materials available it was understood that there would have to be priorities and precedence was given to Sardinia. This decision meant that it was not until March 1943 that the Italians made a concerted effort to reinforce the coastal defences of Sicily. In this task they were aided by German engineers who arrived in the spring of the year and who had themselves been involved in the construction of the Atlantic Wall. Their Italian counterparts, some of whom had been on a fact-finding mission to a number of German coastal positions in France, were keen to create their own version of this great bulwark, but shortages made this difficult and efforts to improve and extend the existing fortifications were disappointing. The three naval bases on Sicily (Augusta, Palermo and Syracuse) were well fortified and were fitted with large-calibre guns, but the situation was very different around potential landing sites. The defences were thinly dispersed and those that existed often lacked weapons and camouflage. There was little in the way of barbed wire, mines or beach obstacles and aerial reconnaissance of one of the British landing beaches prior to the invasion showed a party of bathers.

The lack of beach defences was in part the result of a lack of time and materials, but was also partly the result of Italian strategy. The Italian Commando Supreme was of the view that the Allies would attack on a broad front and as such there was limited value in expending a great amount of effort on beach defences. Indeed, General Roatta,[5] the commander of Italian forces on the Island, planned to construct a belt of

BELOW The coastal defences of Sicily were patchy, but the Italians had fortified key locations like the capital, Palermo. Here a World War I-vintage gun is located in an open position covered with a camouflage net. The gun is a 152mm semi-mobile Canone da 152/45 S 1911. (TM30-246 *Tactical Interpretation of Air Photos 1954*, Figure 625)

---

[4] C. Molony, op. cit., p.37.
[5] He was replaced after only a few months by General Guzzoni.

fortifications and obstacles 19–24km inland – out of the range of Allied ships. These defences were designed to contain any Allied landing until the direction of the main thrust became evident and then the mobile reserve would be employed to decisively defeat them. The Germans, by contrast, believed that the only way to defeat an invasion was to hit the enemy when they were most vulnerable and that was when they were coming ashore. In the end the arguments proved academic. The incomplete beach defences did little to stem the Allied landings and the belt of fortifications to the rear seems to have progressed little further than a line on a map.

Having secured their beachheads, the Allies pressed inland. With no prospect of repelling the enemy invasion the Italo-German force had little choice but to make a fighting retreat and now pinned their faith on a series of defensive 'lines' that it was hoped would stall the enemy advance sufficiently long to enable an orderly evacuation of the island. The term 'line' is somewhat misleading as these were not continuous belts of fortifications but rather were often simply naturally strong defensive positions that were strengthened with mines and fieldworks or demolitions.

The first of these 'lines' was the Hauptkampflinie (main defence line), which ran from San Stefano on the northern coast to Nicosia and then south-east to a point just south of Catania and essentially formed the base of a triangle with Messina at the apex. Behind this was the Etna Line (or Old Hube Line), which, as its name suggests, was constructed around the dormant volcano and ran from a point north of Acireale in front of Aderno and Troina to the coast at San Fratello. The troops manning defensive positions along the line would resist until they were in danger of being overrun or encircled before withdrawing along pre-arranged routes to the next position. There were four of these each with shorter bases that required fewer troops to defend; the surplus troops were to be evacuated to the mainland. The first of these was the 'New Hube Line', but there was seemingly no agreed set of names for the remainder and nor is it clear who fixed the lines.

The series of defensive lines enabled the German forces on Sicily to successfully evacuate the island across the Straits of Messina to the relative safety of mainland Italy. But the success of the operation could not disguise the fact that the Axis forces had been defeated, and soon after Italy surrendered. No longer able to rely on their ally the Germans now anticipated pulling back to a defensive line running roughly from Pisa to Rimini. However, haggling over the Italian peace terms delayed the Allied occupation of Italy and gave Hitler the chance to reconsider his strategy. There was already some debate about where the outer boundary of the Third Reich should be and the Allies' prevarication offered a golden opportunity to set it at the furthest extent possible. Hitler was convinced and rushed 16 divisions south.

These units prepared to repel any invasion force and when the Americans landed at Salerno in September 1943 they were almost driven back into the sea. This success convinced Hitler that there was merit in fighting for Italy and Kesselring, the commander of German forces in Italy, planned to construct a series of delaying positions south of Rome. This strategy had much to commend it, and was not simply based on Hitler's 'psychological inability to surrender territory'.[6] Firstly, the Italian Peninsula was much narrower at this point and would need fewer divisions to defend it and, secondly, it would prevent the Allies capturing the symbolically important city of Rome, along with its airfields.

Before explaining these lines in detail it is worthwhile providing a little background information. Firstly, as in Sicily, the term 'line' is something of a misnomer. A line could be a rallying position, a delaying position, or a position

---

[6] W. Jackson, *The Mediterranean and Middle East, Vol. VI, Victory in the Mediterranean, Part II, June to October 1944* (HMSO: London, 1987), p.9.

for protracted defence. Each of these in turn would be fortified according to its role. The rallying position might simply have been a naturally strong defensive position like a river or a mountain range. A delaying position might have some additional fieldworks, while a position for protracted defence might have had some 'permanent' defences and be built in some depth. Secondly, there is some confusion about the names of the various lines, which is not helped by the fact that certain names were used twice, and by the Germans propensity to change them. To confuse the situation still further the Allies and Germans often used different names for the same positions. A detailed, but not exhaustive, list of the different lines is provided later in the book.

Initially the defensive lines were identified using the German military phonetic alphabet, for example, the A, A1 and B lines, but later they were given proper names, although often still having the same first letter. The first of these lines was the Viktor Line (A and A1 Lines), which followed the Volturno, Calore and Biferno rivers to Termoli on the Adriatic. Running parallel to this, some 16km to the rear, was the Barbara Line. Both of these lines took advantage of natural features with only light fieldworks constructed, and were simply designed to slow the Allied advance to allow time for the completion of defences further north.

Further to the rear again was the Bernhardt Line (also known as the Rheinhardt or Reinhard Line), which broadly followed the Sangro and Gargliano rivers from Fossacesia to Minturno. This had initially been referred to as the B Line and still followed part of the original line. To begin with it was also only considered as a holding line with light fieldworks, but the decision by Hitler to stand and fight in Italy meant that further work was undertaken and it was reclassified as a permanent position. However, the defences were not uniform and the Eighth Army breached the weaker eastern end of the line at the end of 1943 and a further position – the Foro Line – was established running along the Foro River. By contrast the western end of the Bernhardt Line was particularly strong, especially across the mouth of the Liri Valley where a switch position known as the Gustav Line was constructed.

The defences of the Gustav Line stretched from Monte Cairo in the north along the high ground to Monte Cassino, then along the east bank of the river Rapido before following the eastern face of the Aurunci Mountains. The most strongly fortified section of the line was around the town of Cassino. The Rapido River, with its steep banks and swiftly flowing current, was in itself a formidable obstacle, but on the eastern bank it had been reinforced by a thick and continuous network of wire and minefields, while on the German side carefully sited weapons' positions and deep shelters to protect the defenders against air and artillery bombardment had been constructed. Additionally, the whole of the fortified zone was covered by mortar and artillery fire, which could be brought to bear with great accuracy from observation posts on the mountains that overlooked the valley from north and south. Armour was kept to the rear for counterattacking or used as static strongpoints.

In December 1943, the Germans began to build a reserve position known variously as the Führerriegel (Hitler Line), or latterly in German communications as the Sengerriegel,[7] 13km to

BELOW An *MG Panzernest* that formed part of the Gustav Line defences is removed from where it had been buried. An M32 tank recovery vehicle, more used to towing tanks, is used to transport the nest. (US National Archives, 329835)

---

[7] Following the Anzio landings in January 1944 its name was changed to the Sengerriegel, after Fridolin von Senger und Etterlin, the commander of XIV Panzer Corps, who was responsible for the defence of the Liri Valley at that time, because the collapse of a line bearing Hitler's name, it was believed, would be seized on by Allied propagandists.

RIGHT Before the Allied invasion of Sicily the Italians went to some lengths to fortify the coast. Here a series of pillboxes have been constructed to protect the coast road near Gela. (B. Lowry)

the rear of the Gustav Line. This line ran from Piedimonte, on the lower slopes of the Cairo Massif, to Aquino and then Pontecorvo, and from there via Fondi and Terracina to the sea. Again the most heavily defended section of the line covered the Liri Valley, essentially from Piedimonte to Pontecorvo.

Unlike the Gustav Line, the Hitler Line was not a naturally strong defensive position, and instead relied on an elaborate system of defences constructed by the Organization Todt. The defensive belt was between 500 and 1,000m deep. Its main strength lay in its anti-tank defences, which consisted of an anti-tank ditch and extensive minefields covered by anti-tank guns. These included emplaced Panther turrets supported by two or three towed Pak 38 or Pak 40 guns. Approximately 25 self-propelled guns gave depth to the position and also provided a counterattack capability. All told there were some 62 anti-tank guns covering the 5km front. In support of these anti-tank defences the infantry were provided with deep bunkers built of steel and concrete, each with room for 20 men, which gave them shelter against artillery fire and which were connected with one or two covered emplacements, each mounting a machine gun. Additionally, a large number of semi-mobile armoured pillboxes or 'crabs' were installed behind the anti-tank ditch and barbed-wire entanglements. The whole line was covered by approximately 150 artillery pieces together with a considerable number of *Nebelwerfer* and mortars.

To prevent these elaborate defences being outflanked a series of defences at the western end of the Hitler Line were planned, running from Sant' Oliva through Esperia and then to Formia on the coast. This was known as the Dora Line. However, Kesselring and his senior commanders had largely neglected these defences because they considered the Aurunci and Ausonia mountains to be all but impenetrable. As a result the extension consisted of little more than minefields and a few simple earthworks dug to block the important roads and tracks. Covering the approaches to the Dora Line, and designed to bar the Ausonia Valley, was the Orange Line, which ran from the Liri River to Monte Civita, but it was similarly neglected.[8]

BELOW Two Allied soldiers consider the all-round observation afforded by the concrete machine-gun nest in the Hitler Line. Metal hooks set in the roof were used to secure the camouflage net. The timbered entranceway is visible in the foreground leading to the communication trench. (Imperial War Museum, NA 15853)

Behind the Hitler Line, and the last major defensive position before Rome, was the Caesar Line. The main portion of the line ran from the coast just north of the Anzio bridgehead via the Alban Hills to Valmontone with the main fortifications concentrated on the coastal strip, Route 6 and a number of other minor roads that led to Rome. The defences were cleverly sited to take advantage of the natural defensive features,

---

[8] The Bernhardt and Gustav lines, and later the Hitler Line, were loosely referred to by the Allies as the Winter Line.

ADRIATIC SEA

Heinrich Line
Albert Line
*Potenza*
Macerata
Perugia
San Benetto del Tronto
Line E
Ascoli
Teramo
A
Terni
Caesar Line
Pescara
Foro Line
Rieti
P
L'Aquila
Chieti
Dora Line
*Tevere*
P
Bernhardt Line
Advanced Sangro Line
E
Barbara Line
Sulmona
Viktor Line
N
*Tiber*
ROME
*Liri*
San Severo
Manfredonia
'O' Line
Campagna
Switch Line
Frosinone
Isernia
Campobasso
Foggia
N
*Cervaro*
Caesar Line
Cassino
Bari
Anzio
Latina
Orange Line
*Volturno*
*Ofanto*
Hitler Line
Dora Line
I
Gustav Line
Bernhardt Line
Caserta
Benevento
N
Brindisi
Barbara Line
Avellino
Viktor Line
Naples
E
Matera
'O' Line
Salerno
Potenza
S
Taranto
*Agri*

Strait of Otranto

TYRRHENIAN
SEA

Cosenza

Catanzaro

MEDITERRANEAN
SEA

Messina

Palermo

*Mount
Etna*
New Hube Line
Etna Line
SICILY
Catania
Hauptkampflinie

N

Syracuse

Ragusa

MEDITERRANEAN
SEA

| 0 | | 50 miles |
| 0 | | 100km |

11

RIGHT An excellent view of one of the supporting Pak 40 anti-tank guns that protected the flanks of the Panther turrets. The Panther turret in the rear was destroyed by tanks of 51 RTR during the battle for the Hitler Line, May 1944. (Canadian National Archives, PA 114912)

but resources – materials, men and time – were scarce and they were far from complete when the Allies attacked.

Not surprisingly the Caesar Line did little more than delay the Allied advance and on 5 June the Americans entered Rome. There was now only one major prepared defensive position before the Alps and that was the Gothic Line. Preparation of this position had begun when Italy surrendered and had continued intermittently thereafter, but it was not until June 1944 that work began in earnest.

The lack of progress prompted Hitler to change the name of the position from the Gothic Line to the Green Line. The original title was considered too pretentious and gave the impression that a strong fortified position existed, which was not the case. If the line was to be of 'fortress standard', as Hitler hoped, more time would be needed to complete the defences and that meant that Kesselring's forces would have to continue to fight further south. This would not only buy valuable time to finish the work but would also deny the Allies new air bases and limit the room they had to launch an amphibious operation from Italy, perhaps against the Balkans.

To realize these aims a further series of lines was established. The first of these was the Dora Line, which was a rallying position north of the Eternal City that ran from Orbetello to Terni, then via Pieti and Aquinta to the eastern end of the Caesar Line. Behind this was 'Line E', which was a delaying position designed to slow the Allies before they reached the main line of defence – the Albert Line. This snaked from Ancona on the Adriatic to Perugia and then on to Lake Trasimeno before following the Ombrone River to the coast.

Behind the Albert Line were further delaying positions on the west coast, notably the Anton and Lilo lines that protected Leghorn and Siena respectively. And behind these lines, designed to protect Florence and the Arno crossings, were 'the Olga and Lydia lines [which] ran from Montopoli in the west to Figline on Highway 69, with the Paula and Mädchen line in echelon behind them on the line La Romola to Impruneta.'[9] These positions, together with the Georg Line, a further intermediate withdrawal line that covered Volterra and Arezzo, would allow the German forces to fall back in good order to the next, and last, defensive line before the Green Line, the Heinrich Line. This started at Pisa on the west coast and ran along the north bank of the Arno and followed the line of the Apennines until it reached the coast at Senigallia.

---

[9] M. Tillotson, 'Umbria and Tuscany in the wake of the Allies', *The Times*, 6 October 2004, p.65

Immediately in front of the Green Line were two further defensive positions that formed the outer bulwarks of the main line. The Vorfeld Line was a deep outpost zone 'in which all roads and buildings were to be demolished and "lavishly" mined.'[10] It started at Fano on the Adriatic and followed the Metauro to its source in the Apennines and then on to a point just east of Florence where it effectively merged with the Heinrich position; behind this was a further intermediate position called the Red Line.[11]

ABOVE The view through the aperture of a German pillbox located near San Giuliano. It shows how the position dominated the twisting section of road in front. (US National Archives, 359086)

The 'Green Line' in actual fact consisted of two separate positions. Green I ran from Pesaro in the east to La Spezia in the west and Green II ran parallel to the first some 16km to the rear, but only as far as the Futa Pass where the two merged. At the rear edge of the Green Line was the Rimini Line. As its name suggests it was anchored on the Adriatic at Rimini and followed the Ausa River to the principality of San Marino. The value of these lines had long been recognized because they offered the last chance of a defensive action on a comparatively short front while at the same time taking advantage of the Apennine Mountains, which at this point stretched from the Ligurian Sea almost to the Adriatic. If there was time to properly fortify and man these positions it was hoped that an attack on them would so weaken the enemy in a battle of attrition that further enemy operations would be much reduced or have to be cancelled completely. Moreover, it was important that the Apennine position was held because behind it lay the Plains of Lombardy. This flat expanse was perfect for large-scale operations and was rich in agriculture. An Allied breakthrough here would mean that extra food supplies would need to be provided for German forces in Italy and would also mean the loss of the industrial output from the Milan–Turin industrial basin.

The ramifications were unthinkable but eminently possible and even before the completion of the Apennine position a final defensive position had been identified – the Voralpenstellung – and in front of this a series of rallying and delaying lines were instituted. These intermediate positions were established along the line of the numerous fast-flowing rivers that ran from the Apennines, across the path of the Allies' advance, to the Adriatic. On the Savio River was the Erika Line and behind that on the Ronco was the Gudrun position, which protected Forlì and blocked the via Emilia (Route 9), one of the main arterial roads. Next came the Augsberger Line, which ran along the Montone and Lamone rivers and protected Ravenna. After that was the Irmgard Line, which followed the Senio, the Laura Line running along the Santerno, the Paula Line along the Sillaro and the Anna Line, which hugged the Gaiana.

In October 1944 a further defensive line east of Bologna was established. The Genghis Khan Line, as it was known, ran from Lake Comacchio along the Idice River to the foothills of the Apennines. This formed the forward line of a position that had already been prepared along the Reno River and which was sometimes referred to as the Reno Line.

The last line of defence before the Voralpenstellung was what the Allies referred to as the Venetian or Adige Line and what the Germans called the Red Line. This ran along the Adige River to the southern tip of Lake Garda and was,

[10] W. Jackson, op. cit., p.59.
[11] A name later used for the Venetian Line.

RIGHT The Apennines were an extremely strong natural feature, but the Germans still constructed a series of defences along the range and especially through the many passes. This concrete machine-gun shelter was built to cover the road along the Serchio Valley near Barga. (Imperial War Museum, NA21203)

as one historian described it, 'the glacis protecting the southern wall of his [Hitler's] National Redoubt.'[12]

The Voralpenstellung, or Forward Alpine Defences of the National Redoubt (also known as the Blue Line), was begun in July 1944 and included in its arsenal coastal artillery taken from the Ligurian Coast. The line ran from the border of Switzerland, across the Julian Alps to Monfalcone and was tied in with a series of defensive lines that ran along the Brenta, Piave, Tagliamento and Isonzo rivers that were to block the so-called Ljubljana Gap. The defences on the last two rivers were much more advanced and there were plans to emplace Panther tank turrets here in much the same way that they had been in the Hitler and Green lines.

Technically speaking the National Redoubt, or Alpenfestung (Alpine Fortress), lay outside of Italy and as such outside the scope of this book, but it warrants a brief mention for completeness. The *Gauleiter* for the Austrian province had floated the idea of a last redoubt in the Tyrolean Alps. Some work on the defences did begin but shortages of men and material, which had bedevilled previous attempts to build defensive lines in Italy, were now more acute and only a few fortifications on the Austro-Swiss border were completed.

Also worthy of mention are the fortifications constructed by the Italians and inherited by the Germans. Before World War I, defences had been constructed on the Ligurian Coast to meet the possible threat from France, but when Italy joined the Triple Entente this threat disappeared and in World War I these defences were largely abandoned and the weapons transferred to the front with Austria-Hungary. After the war the coastal defences were steadily improved with the building of a series of medium artillery batteries. These were subjected to a number of attacks by French and British naval forces in the early part of World

[12] W. Jackson, *The Battle for Italy* (Harper and Row: New York, 1967), p.295.

AUSTRIA

•Berne

SWITZERLAND

LIECHTENSTEIN

Adige

Bolzano

Voralpenstellung

ALPS

Lake
Maggiore

Lake
Como

Adda

Trent

Brenta

Astico

Piave

Pordenone

Trieste

•Aosta

Oglio

Lake
Garda

Vicenza

Treviso

ADRIATIC SEA

Ticino

•Milan

Brescia

Verona

Padua

Venice

Turin•

Po

Adda

Pavia

Chiese

Adige

Rovigo

Venetian Line

•Cremona

Mantua

Po

Piacenza

Po

Ferrara

Trebbia

Parma

Reno

Anna Line

Genghis Khan Line

Irmgard Line

•Parma

Modena

Augsberger Line

APPENNINES

Reggio Emilia

Bologna

Ravenna

Gudrun Line

Mt S Michele Line

Imola

Erika Line

Genoa

Genghis Khan Line

Faenza

Paula Line

Forli

Cesena

Rimini Line

Laura Line

Green II Line

Green II Line

Massa Line

Rimini

Green I Line

Spezia

Massa

SAN
MARINO

Pesaro

Red Line

Green I Line

Vorfeld Line

Pistoia

Fano

Lucca

Florence

Senigallia

Massa

Paula Line

Pisa

Metauro

Fossombrone

Ancona

Heinrich Line

Arno

Olga & Lydia Lines

Heinrich Line

Albert Line

Leghorn

Elsa

Georg Line

Arezzo

Macerata

Lilo Line

Siena

Lake
Trasimeno

Potenza

Perugia

FRANCE

MONACO

LIGURIAN
SEA

Anton Line

Foligno

Line E

Elba

Tiber

Terni

Albert Line

Grosseto

Lake
Bolsena

Rieti

Line E

Viterbo

Dora Line

Dora Line

Tevere

CORSICA

ROME

Campagna Switch Line

MEDITERRANEAN
SEA

TYRRHENIAN
SEA

Caesar Line

Latina

Anzio

N

SARDINIA

| 0 | | 50 miles |
|---|---|---|
| 0 | | 100km |

War II and the weakness of the defences highlighted, in particular the lack of any large-calibre artillery pieces. This shortcoming was rectified with the building of a number of large coastal batteries, but ironically these were not tested before the Italian surrender and the defences fell into the hands of the Germans. Some renovation and improvement work was undertaken by the Organization Todt, much of which was completed in a burst of activity in the spring of 1944 when there was a very real possibility of an Allied landing. This principally consisted of work to build obstacles and casemates to enfilade the beaches and also efforts to strengthen open positions against air attack. As it transpired the Allies landed in southern France and the defences of the rather grandly named Ligurian Wall were abandoned and the garrisons were relocated to France or to the Green Line. Ultimately the only action the defences saw was against local partisans and in April 1945 the troops that remained surrendered to the Americans.

The other major defensive position inherited from the Italians was the Vallo Alpino. Ironically much of this had been constructed to deter an attack by Germany and as such most of the defences were of little use against an enemy attacking from the south. However, this was not true of the Ingrid Line, which ran along the Italian border with the former Yugoslavia. The defences here were strengthened by the Organization Todt with the addition of standard shelters and fieldworks against a possible Allied invasion of the Balkans, or, as became increasingly likely, a possible Soviet attack.

ABOVE In order to safely store their ammunition for the weapons employed along the Gothic Line the Germans blasted a number of caves in the mountains. This cave was located near Castiglione Dei Pepoli. It was 5m deep and strengthened with timber props. It was used to house mortar rounds, as shown, and 170mm artillery shells. (Imperial War Museum, NA19204)

RIGHT An Italian concrete pillbox constructed near San Giuliano. The position has a number of apertures that gave it good all-round observation. Rocks have been stacked in front to provide added protection and for camouflage. (US National Archives, 196449)

# The principles of defence

After three years of successful campaigning, at the end of 1942 Hitler's ground forces suffered their first major reverse at El Alamein and thereafter they were forced on to the defensive. However, Hitler was determined not to surrender any of the hard-won gains and ordered the construction of a series of defensive lines built, whenever possible, using the principle of defence in depth. The idea had been developed in World War I and was used on the Western Front in the construction of the Hindenburg Line. In the interwar period the principle was again adopted in the building of the West Wall. Now in Italy, where the topography was ideally suited to the defence, there was a good opportunity to use the technique again, both at a strategic and an operational level. Strategically, the Germans planned to build a series of defensive lines across the peninsula and throughout its length. These were designed to stop or at least slow the Allied advance. This would keep them as far as possible from Germany's border and at the same time limit their opportunities to launch new air, land and amphibious operations.

At an operational level each of the lines, and certainly those designed for protracted defence, were constructed in depth. At the leading edge were minefields, barbed wire and anti-tank ditches. Behind these defences were machine-gun and anti-tank positions that covered the line throughout its length. Further to the rear artillery, rockets and mortars were registered on the expected routes of advance. The idea was to separate the infantry and the armour and to isolate the attackers from their own forces, so making them vulnerable to counterattack by reserves held in the rear, sheltered against the preliminary air and artillery bombardment, and earmarked for the purpose.

## Gustav Line

Defensive lines had already been used in Sicily and in the early part of the campaign on the mainland. However, these lines tended not to be continuous and they certainly were not constructed in depth. The first real example was the Gustav Line. Here the Rapido River provided a difficult natural obstacle for any attacker to negotiate and this had been strengthened with the addition of mines and barbed wire. Behind these machine guns had been sited to provide interlocking fields of fire, especially around the most likely avenues of approach. Frequently these were housed in armoured pillboxes, which were known to the Germans as *MG Panzernester* and to the Allies as crabs. These firing positions were often linked to troop shelters at the rear. These were either prefabricated steel shelters or constructed from concrete with some large enough to contain sleeping accommodation for 20 or 30 men. Further to the rear mortars, *Nebelwerfer* and artillery were located to provide indirect fire support.

In the town of Cassino itself and on the surrounding slopes a very different approach had to be adopted. Here the closely packed buildings meant that a traditional defensive position was not possible. Moreover, the heavy fighting and later Allied bombing had flattened many of the buildings. Far from being a

BELOW Two members of the 4th Canadian Anti-Tank Regiment examine a captured *Nebelwerfer*, or 'moaning minnie', so named because of the weird, screeching ululation that the rockets made as they fell. Although not particularly accurate, the *Nebelwerfer* was capable of causing tremendous physical and psychological damage. (Canadian National Archives, PA 169113)

The Hitler Line ran southwards from Piedimonte on the lower slopes of the Cairo massif to Aquino and Pontecorvo, and from there via Fondi and Terracina to the sea. The most heavily defended section of the line covered the Liri Valley and part of this is portrayed here, specifically the defences covering the strategically important Route 6, showing how it would have looked prior to the battle in May 1944. Across the whole of the front minefields were enclosed within a double-apron barbed-wire fence. Some 70m behind the wire entanglements was an anti-tank ditch. This had been blown electronically with demolition charges at about 5m intervals. Covering the anti-tank ditch and the barbed wire were slit trenches. These were dug in a zigzag pattern so that troops were less exposed to flanking fire. In addition to the fieldworks, reinforced concrete light machine-gun emplacements were constructed along with *MG Panzernest*

armoured pillboxes. These were buried in the ground so that only a small section of the top was visible. Two Panther turrets were also located in this section of the line to counter the threat from Allied armour and these were supplemented with either 75mm Pak 40 or 50mm Pak 38 guns, which were echeloned to the rear of the turret in a series of spearheads. In addition to the static anti-tank positions a number of self-propelled guns, including 88mm Hornets, were employed. These gave depth to the position and could also be used for counter attacks. Situated just behind the main defences were a number of dugouts. These provided shelter for the troops manning the positions against enemy bombardment. Further back still *Nebelwerfer* rocket launchers were positioned to provide indirect fire support. Along the line numerous other mounds and pits were dug. These were often either uncompleted positions or dummy positions designed to confuse the enemy.

handicap for the paratroopers assigned to this section of the line this was a positive boon, because, as the Germans knew from bitter experience at Stalingrad, rubble makes a better defensive position than undamaged buildings. Wherever possible shelters were constructed on the ground floor or in the cellars of buildings. These shelters were walled and roofed with heavy logs or girders and covered with a thick layer of rubble, which made them impervious to direct hits even from large-calibre artillery shells. Tanks and self-propelled guns were also positioned inside the shells of buildings as improvised strong points and proved extremely effective.

# Hitler Line

To the rear of the Gustav Line was the Hitler Line. This was not a naturally strong defensive position and as such German engineers went to great lengths to construct a continuous line of defences in some depth. With little time to complete the work a simple anti-tank ditch was blasted along the length of the line. In front of this was a thick band of barbed wire sown with mines. Behind these passive defences were machine-gun positions and, for the first time, Panther turrets mounted on steel shelters were used. These were positioned in a single defensive line in such a way that they were able to cover the line throughout its length. They were deployed in a series of spearheads. At the tip of each spear there was a Panther turret and echeloned back on either side were two or three towed 75mm or 50mm anti-tank guns. The turrets were located so that they commanded the approaches to the line with particularly long fields of fire to their front where trees had been cut down to approximately 45cm from the ground. They had more restricted fields of fire to the flank and particularly the rear, and towed anti-tank guns covered these weak spots. These were generally employed in pairs approximately 150–200m behind or to the flank of the turrets and were often hidden behind houses, in sunken roads or in thick cover. Some 25 self-propelled guns were also positioned along this same line with some held further to the rear to give depth to the defences, or to provide the punch for any counterattack.

BELOW An example of a reinforced shelter constructed inside a house in the Hitler Line. This example was constructed on piers which shouldered steel girders and logs. On top of this framework masonry and rubble were poured to a thickness of some 65cm. One of the entrances to the house was blocked with barrels filled with stones. (Public Record Office, WO291/1315)

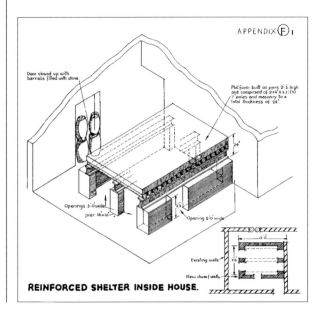

APPENDIX (F) 1

Door closed up with barrels filled with stone.

Platform built on piers 2·3 high and composed of 9x4"h.s.i.(3) 7" poles and masonry to a Total thickness of 24".

Openings 3'0 wide
pier 16'x10'

Opening 2'0 wide

Existing walls

New outer walls

**REINFORCED SHELTER INSIDE HOUSE.**

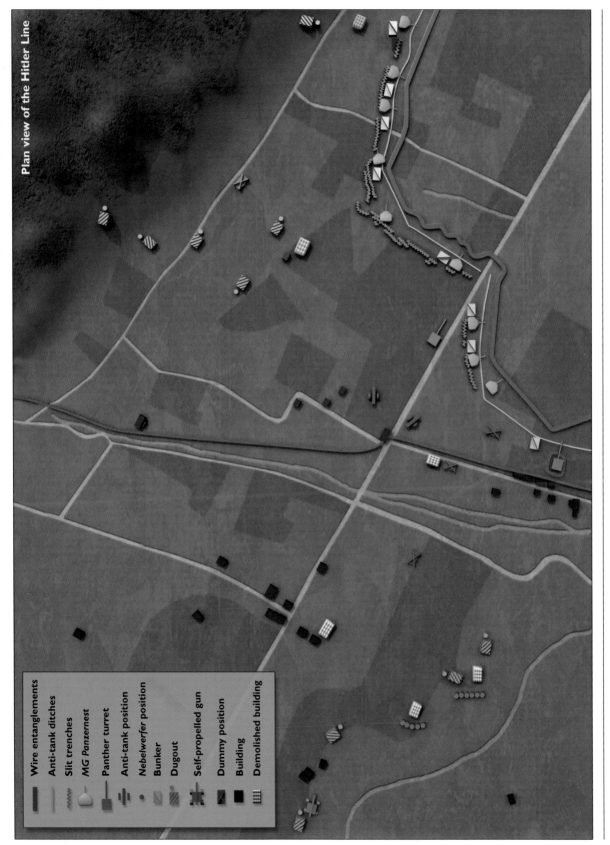

Plan view of the Hitler Line

Wire entanglements
Anti-tank ditches
Slit trenches
MG Panzernest
Panther turret
Anti-tank position
Nebelwerfer position
Bunker
Dugout
Self-propelled gun
Dummy position
Building
Demolished building

ABOVE One of the *Nashorn* self-propelled guns armed with an 88mm gun being inspected by Canadian infantrymen (their unit badges obliterated by the censor). This example was employed in the Hitler Line. They were cleverly concealed, often behind buildings, as here, and would pick off a target before withdrawing to another position. (Canadian National Archives, PA 130348)

BELOW American soldiers inspect a section of the anti-tank ditch of the Gothic Line. The technique for revetting the sides is clearly evident with uprights held in place by wire securing the brushwood behind. (US National Archives, 1946245)

## Caesar Line

The Caesar Line was to be constructed in much the same way as the Gustav and Hitler Lines, but because resources had been diverted south, work on the line was far from finished by the end of May. The defences protecting Rome were largely complete though with thick bands of barbed wire and mines laid to block the most favourable routes of approach. Covering these defences were machine-gun and anti-tank positions; mortars, *Nebelwerfer* and artillery provided indirect fire support. However, as General von Mackensen, the commander of Fourteenth Army, was quick to point out, 'the Caesar Line was suitable for no more than a delaying action'.[13]

## Gothic Line

The Gothic Line, or Green Line as it was later known, was the last major defensive line before the Alps. The Italian Army had identified the potential of a line running roughly from Pisa to Rimini and the merits of such a position were not lost on the OKW. Work on the defences had begun in late 1943, but had been suspended to concentrate resources on the Gustav and the Hitler lines. Only in the summer of 1944 did work resume.

The position was immensely strong, incorporating as it did the mass of the Apennines and a number of rivers that had their source in the mountains and flowed to the Adriatic. There were weak points, the principal one being the coastal plain around Pesaro, and this is where the bulk of the defences were concentrated. This was the responsibility of von Vietinghoff's Tenth Army and in this section of the line alone it was planned to lay more than 200,000 mines (although by the end of August 1944 less than half had been completed – 73,000 *Tellerminen* and 23,000 *Schrapnellminen*). A continuous anti-tank ditch almost 10km long had been dug and almost 120,000m of barbed wire had been used. Covering the line were almost 2,500 machine-gun positions, including *MG Panzernester* and PzKpfw (*Panzerkampfwagen*) I and II turrets adapted for static employment. Panther turrets were also used with particular concentrations in the section of the line that ran along the Foglia River from Pesaro on the east coast to Montécchio. By the end of August four of these positions had been completed in this section of the line with a further 18 under construction. In addition seven disabled Panther tanks had been dug in with another one being installed. There were also almost 500 positions for anti-tank guns and *Nebelwerfer* and some 2,500 dugouts of various types, including Organization Todt steel shelters.

There had been little time to build the defences in any great depth and indeed Green II was little more than a reconnoitred line on German staff maps, although its natural features were strong. Panther turrets were installed to the rear, but this seems to have been the only attempt to provide depth to the position. As for possible outflanking manoeuvres, on the Adriatic Coast, which Kesselring regarded as the most vulnerable of the two, dragon's teeth were constructed on the beaches, laced with barbed wire and mines, to counter another Allied landing. Large concrete bunkers were also constructed to house coastal artillery.

---

[13] E. Fisher, *Cassino to the Alps* (Center for Military History: Washington, 1977), p.156.

The western section of the Gothic Line was dominated by the Apennine Mountains and as such offered fewer opportunities for an Allied breakthrough. The weakest point was along Route 65 through the Futa Pass and it is here that Lemelsen, the new commander of Fourteenth Army, concentrated his defences. The outpost zone consisted of minefields, an anti-tank ditch and barbed-wire entanglements. Behind these were fire trenches that covered the line throughout its length. Further to the rear were concrete pillboxes, troop shelters and the much-feared emplaced Panther turrets. One was installed close to the village of Santa Lucia, guarding the long anti-tank ditch dug a few kilometres south of the pass, and another on the pass itself. Similar defences were also constructed on Highway 6620 to the west, the Prato–Bologna road, and to protect Il Giogo Pass to the east, although both lacked Panther turrets. A Panther turret was installed at the Poretta Pass to protect Route 64 above Pistoia.

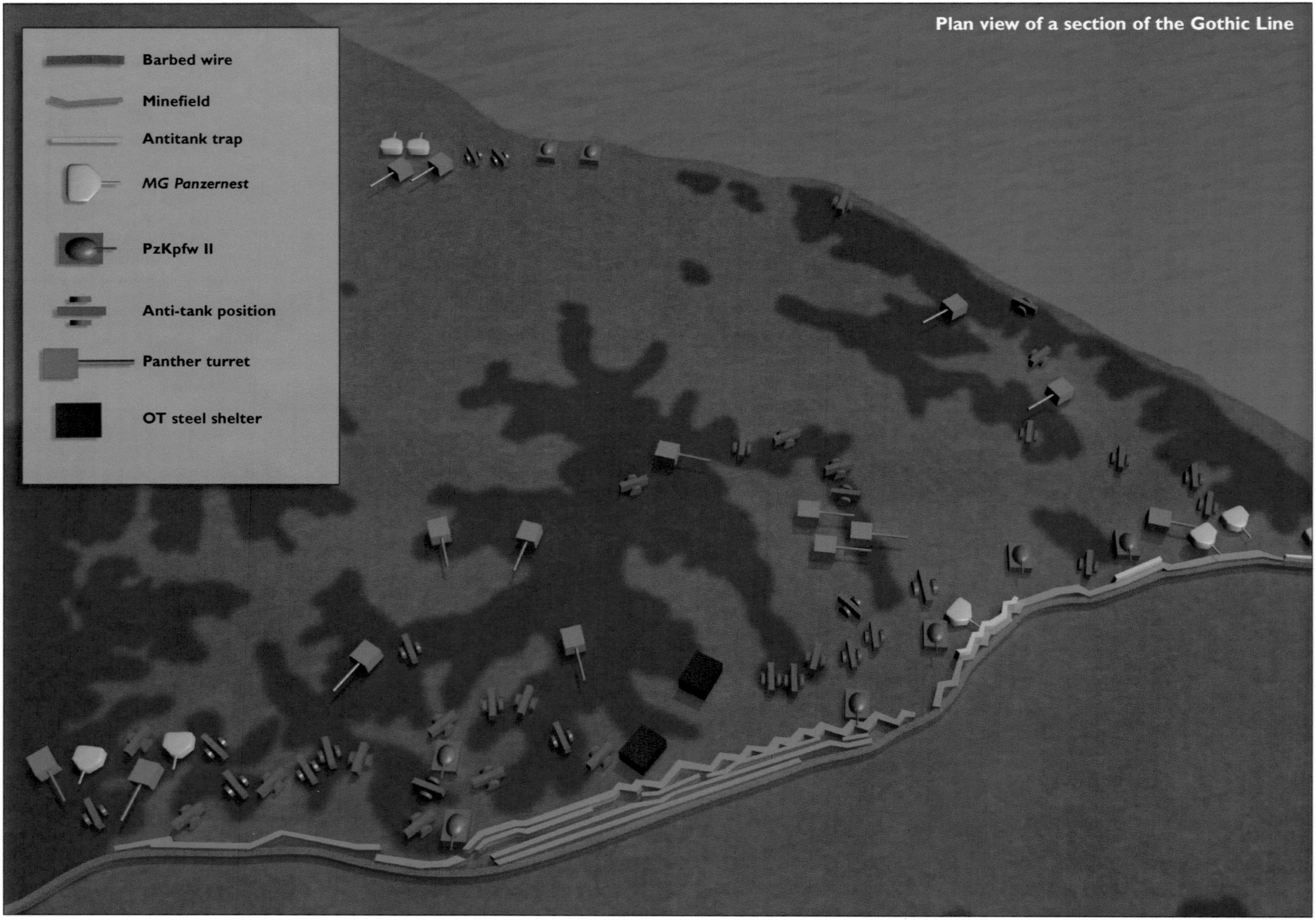

Plan view of a section of the Gothic Line

Barbed wire
Minefield
Antitank trap
*MG Panzernest*
PzKpfw II
Anti-tank position
Panther turret
OT steel shelter

OPPOSITE **Plan view of a section of the Gothic Line**
This plate depicts a small section of the Gothic Line that ran from Pesaro on the coast inland to Tomba di Pesaro and to the rear to Cattolica. The defences are depicted as they were planned in the autumn of 1944 and demonstrate the German concept of defence in depth. At the front of the position were barbed-wire entanglements and mines, which would have been laid forward of and amongst the wire. Behind the wire was an anti-tank trap. This was dug to a depth of 2.5m, which, with the spoil, meant that the overall depth was 3m; it was also 4.5m wide. It was revetted with logs and brushwood secured with anchor wires. Covering the passive defences were a number of *MG Panzernester* and old PzKpfw II tank turrets mounted on specially designed shelters. To provide anti-tank defence 8.8cm and 7.5cm Paks were employed. The guns were employed in simple open emplacements. Slightly further to the rear were a number of emplaced Panther turrets mounted on OT steel shelters. A number of immobilized Panther tanks were also simply buried in the ground and used as improvised fixed fortifications. To provide protection for the troops OT steel shelters, similar to those mounting the Panther turrets, were buried in the ground.

## Voralpenstellung

The last of the major defensive lines was the Voralpenstellung, which was constructed in north-eastern Italy to block the so-called 'Ljubljana Gap'. According to German files this position was to be heavily fortified, with plans to install 30 tank turrets mounting machine guns, 37 Panther tank turrets, 100 Italian M42 tank turrets fitted with a German 3.7cm Kwk and 100 P40 turrets fitted with a German 7.5cm Kwk. It was also envisaged that a significant number of tank guns fitted to improvised mounts would be installed. However, it is unclear how many of these defences were completed. Certainly a number of the Panther turrets were being installed by January 1945, but others were destroyed or delayed in transit.

## Achilles heel

For all the effort that went into the construction of the various defensive lines in Italy, they failed to stop the Allied advance. This judgement might seem harsh, because they certainly helped to delay the progress of Fifteenth Army Group. However, it must be remembered that Alexander's forces were never significantly larger than those fielded by Kesselring and he certainly did not enjoy the 3:1 advantage that was considered necessary for a successful attack on such prepared positions. And yet in spite of this fact the Allies were still able to breach the defences. True, Alexander could field more armour and artillery but these advantages were of less significance in a mountainous country like Italy. The same cannot be said of air power and this highlights one of the major shortcomings of such defences. They are by their very nature static and therefore vulnerable to attack from the air. Allied tactical and strategic bombing raids meant that work on the defences was constantly interrupted by direct interdiction or by delays in the supply of materials. This, together with sabotage and a less than committed workforce, meant that many of the defences were not complete or were sub-standard. Moreover, unfettered air observation meant that Allied ground forces always had good intelligence on enemy defences, despite the fact that much of the work was undertaken at night and camouflaged during the day.

BELOW An aerial view of a section of the Voralpenstellung east of Gorizia. The arrows indicate anti-tank gun emplacements. 'A' shows a belt of dragon's teeth. 'B', 'C' and 'D' are anti-tank ditches. (TM30-246 *Tactical Interpretation of Air Photos 1954*, Figure 208)

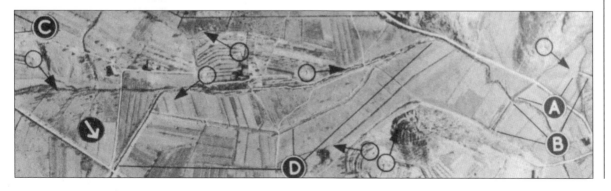

The poor state of the defences also undoubtedly lowered the troop's morale. Goebbel's Propaganda Ministry made much of the strength of the defences, but its highly coloured description of the defences often did not match the reality. Indeed Engineer General Bessell, when taking over responsibility for the Gothic Line at the end of June, noted that

> The line was without depth, lacked emplacements for heavy weapons, and was little more than a chain of light machine-gun posts. Fields of fire had not been cleared, anti-tank obstacles were rudimentary and the 'main line' ran across forward slopes. Indeed, von Vietinghoff after inspecting the line wondered if in fact they had been done by soldiers.[14]

And even where the defences had been completed there were often insufficient troops and weapons to employ in the positions. As Machiavelli famously stated, 'fortresses without good armies are incompetent for defence'. Furthermore, the rigid defences in many respects reduced the scope for the soldier on the ground to use his own initiative that had been such an important part of the German Army's early success.

At a strategic level the major problem with such defensive lines on the Italian Peninsula was that they could be outflanked by amphibious assault. In January 1944 VI (US) Corps landed at Anzio almost unopposed and had the chance of outflanking the Winter Line and capturing Rome. Overcautious commanders on the ground saw this opportunity squandered, but the prospect of a further landing was never far from the mind of German generals. These fears did diminish following Operation *Overlord* in June 1944 and certainly after the landings in southern France in August 1944, because it was recognized that the number of landing craft available to the Allies was finite. However, there was still concern about a possible landing on the Adriatic Coast and as such it was never possible to have complete faith in any defensive line, no matter how strong, for fear of it being outflanked by a landing in the rear.

---

[14] W. Jackson, *The Mediterranean and Middle East, Vol. VI, Victory in the Mediterranean, Part II, June to October 1944* (HMSO: London, 1987), p.60.

# Tour of the sites

Each of the defensive lines built by the Germans in Italy was unique, built as they were to take advantage of natural features specific to that area, but often they shared common characteristics. The outpost zone consisted of passive defences; barbed-wire entanglements, minefields and, where there was no river or similar feature, an anti-tank ditch. Covering the whole were machine-gun positions, often mounted in *MG Panzernester* or tank turrets, and to provide anti-tank defence Panther turrets were installed. Exceptionally, a number of other defences were constructed. Dragon's teeth, which had first been used along the West Wall, were installed along the coast, and further inland large coastal guns were mounted in concrete casemates. Finally, in the last desperate days of the war there were plans to use tank guns mounted on swivel mounts as improvised anti-tank guns.

Two types of mine were employed: *Tellerminen*, which were used against vehicles, and anti-personnel mines. The mines tended to be laid in rectangular blocks to cover expected avenues of attack or, in the case of *Tellerminen*, they were often laid along roads and tracks. The weight of the vehicle would detonate the charge. The same principle applied to the *Schützenmine 42*, or 'Schu Mine', which was one of the most widely used anti-personnel mines. This consisted of a plywood box packed with 200g of TNT. Pressure on the lid would set off the charge. Because it was in a wooden box it was exceptionally difficult to detect. Captured Italian models were also employed and these were equally hard to find in Sicily because of the high iron content in the rock and lava. The *Schrapnellmine*

ABOVE The coast near Ravenna was fortified with pillboxes and protected with wire and, as seen here, dragon's teeth and mines. The mines are probably Italian anti-tank mines in wooden cases and were lifted by sappers to enable an airfield to be constructed nearby. (Imperial War Museum, NA20897)

LEFT An army observation post for a coastal battery (Type 637) positioned on the west coast. This example was only just completed when US forces captured it. The wooden shuttering is still in place on one side and is also evident in the foreground. (US National Archives, 193355)

25

35 was slightly different. This was activated by direct pressure on the head or by use of trip wires. A small charge would then propel the mine into the air where it would explode, scattering shrapnel over a wide area.

Often minefields were enclosed within a double-apron barbed-wire fence. This generally consisted of rows of concertina wire or wire stretched between screw pickets. Behind this, stretched just above the ground, was a broad band of trip wire.

In the absence of a river or similar anti-tank obstacle it was necessary to construct a man-made alternative. In the Hitler and Gothic lines anti-tank traps or *Panzerabwehrgraben* were dug. These varied in length and sophistication. In the Hitler Line this was little more than a consecutive series of craters that had been blown electronically with demolition charges at about 5m intervals. Accordingly, the width of the ditch varied from 7m to 11m and the depth from 2m to 4m. Only in a few places had any additional spadework been done. In a number of instances the explosive charges had not detonated and as a result there were irregular gaps in the ditch. A more elaborate affair was constructed at the eastern end of the Gothic Line running inland from the coast. It was dug to a depth of 2.5m, which with the spoil meant that the overall depth was 3m, and was 4.5m wide. It was revetted with logs and brushwood held in place with anchor wires secured to stakes that were buried to protect them against enemy artillery. For every kilometre dug some 6,200m$^3$ of soil had to be removed.

Covering the outpost zone were a variety of weapons. One worthy of mention because of its uniqueness was the *Abwehrflammenwerfer* 42, which was dug in at ground level in forward posts of the Gothic Line. This weapon was based on a Soviet design first encountered by the Germans in the Stalin Line. The 22.7-litre fuel tank was buried in the ground so that only the nozzle was visible. They were often used in groups spaced 10–25m apart and were ignited by a fuse or a trip wire. This would trigger a 50m jet of flame that lasted 5–10 seconds.

More normally the passive defences were covered by various machine-gun positions, including the *MG Panzernest*. This was developed in the second half of the war and proved invaluable when the German Army was on the retreat. Weighing just less than 3,200kg it could be transported and installed relatively easily and provided valuable protection for the two-man crew against enemy small-arms fire and shrapnel.

The nest was constructed from two steel prefabricated sections that were welded together. The top half contained the aperture for the gun, air vents and the rear entrance hatch, which was hinged at the base. This section was most vulnerable to enemy fire and was cast accordingly with armour around the aperture 13cm thick and 5cm around the sides and the roof. The base of the unit, which was completely below ground, was about 12.5mm thick.

The frontal aperture was divided into two parts: the lower part accommodated the gun barrel and the upper part was for sighting. Two periscopes in the roof

OPPOSITE **A cutaway view of a PzKpfw II turret**
In addition to the heavier Panther turrets, a number of PzKpfw II turrets were installed along the Gothic Line. These turrets were readily available by this stage in the war because it was recognized that the main armament of the PzKpfw II – a 20mm Kwk 30 canon – was hopelessly ineffective against the new generation of Allied armour that included the T-34. The surplus turrets were freed up for use as fixed fortifications and plans for the shelter mounting the PzKpfw II turret were drawn up in December 1942. Eventually, 17 were emplaced in Italy. The plate depicts a PzKpfw II turret captured in the Gothic Line in September 1944. The cutaway view shows

the steps leading from the trench down into the shelter and then the steps leading up into the fighting compartment. This was fitted with wooden duckboards, which served as a makeshift repository for the spent shell cases. Any water that entered the fighting compartment would also collect here before being channelled through a drain to the lower level where the floor was angled at 2 degrees to direct water out of the shelter to the soak away at the entrance. Ammunition was stored in two niches, which were recessed into the wall of the fighting compartment. The turret sat on an octagonal baseplate, which was secured to the top of the shelter by eight bolts.

**A cutaway view of a PzKpfw II turret**

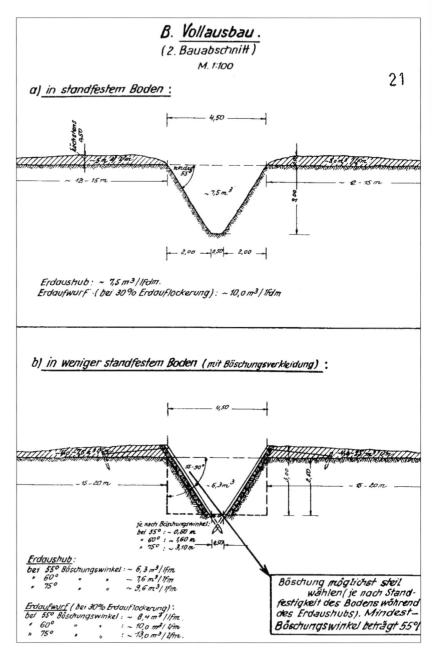

provided further observation. When not in use the aperture could be covered with a shield operated from within the shelter. The relatively small aperture meant that the machine gun had a limited field of fire of approximately 60 degrees. Because of this and because the nest could not be rotated they tended to be used for flanking fire with other positions providing mutual support.

A simple foot-operated ventilation system was provided that used holes at the side of the turret. These also acted as the mounting for an axle. With the nest upside down wheels could be fitted on either side. A limber was attached to the machine-gun embrasure and two further wheels were located in front. This was then hooked up to a tractor and the whole could then be towed.

Machine guns were also fitted in old tank turrets mounted on concrete bunkers. These were built to a standard design. Directly below the turret was the fighting compartment. This was fitted with wooden duckboards, which not only

LEFT An Allied soldier inspects one of the flamethrowers that were used in the Gothic Line. The fuel tank of the *Abwehrflammenwerfer 42* was buried in the ground so that only the nozzle was visible. They were often used in groups and when triggered would project a jet of flame for some 50m. (Imperial War Museum, NA 18338)

improved the crew's footing but also served as a repository for spent machine-gun cases. Any water that entered the fighting compartment would also collect here before being channelled through a drain to the lower level, where the floor was angled at 2 degrees to direct water out of the shelter to the soakaway at the entrance. Access to the fighting compartment was via a flight of steps from the anteroom inside the entrance, which in turn was linked to a revetted trench at the side. This room also housed the hand-operated ventilation system.

Turrets were taken from a number of obsolete German tanks. These included a number of modified PzKpfw I turrets. The original mantlet was removed and replaced with a 20mm-thick plate with openings for the machine gun and the sight. The two vision slits in the turret side were dispensed with and were

LEFT A close-up of an artillery casemate. An American soldier admires the unusual camouflage scheme, which shows more than a little artistic flare. Superficial damage would suggest that the position was involved in some localized fighting or was strafed by Allied aircraft. (US National Archives, 196235)

**A Panther turret installed on the Hitler Line**
Along the length of the Hitler Line, Panther turrets mounted on specially designed shelters were installed. One of these turrets covered the strategically important Route 6, which led from Monte Cassino to Rome. The turret, taken from a Panther Ausf. D tank, was positioned just behind the anti-tank ditch and wire and would have been heavily camouflaged but this has been omitted for clarity. At the front of the position was a shallow sandbag trench that was just deep enough for the gun to be depressed into so that it did not cast a telltale shadow for Allied aircraft to spot. The turret was mounted on an OT steel shelter that was buried in the ground and encased in concrete 1–1.5m thick. The shelter itself was constructed in two parts. The upper box incorporated the turret ball-race and housed the ammunition for the main armament. The lower structure was divided into three compartments. The largest of these was fitted with nine fold-down bunk beds and a stove for heat. In the right-hand rear corner of the compartment there was an escape hatch. The second compartment acted as home for a 2hp motor, together with a dynamo, a storage battery and a compressed air tank. The final compartment was fitted with a steel ladder that linked the upper and lower boxes and also incorporated the main access hatch. From here a revetted trench led away from the shelter. This was 60cm wide and 1.3m deep and ran to an abandoned building located on the Aquino road. Approximately two-thirds of the way along the trench was an ammunition shelter. This was 2.6m square and 1.3m deep and was covered with timber and spoil. This is shown separately in cutaway. All around the position was a barbed-wire fence.

covered by 20mm steel plates which were welded over the openings as ventilation ports. This meant they were much better suited for their new role. A number of PzKpfw II turrets were also used and a similar number of Czech PzKpfw 38(t)s were also made available for use in the Gothic Line (see Table 1).

There were also plans to use large numbers of Italian tank turrets that had fallen into German hands following their occupation of the country. These turrets were to be mounted on specially designed concrete bunkers (although a wooden design was also later developed). There were plans to install 100 P40 turrets and 100 M42 turrets in the Voralpenstellung, but it is unclear as to whether this work was completed. A number of other Italian tanks were simply dug in and used as improvised strongpoints. P40 tanks were used in this way in the Gustav Line and at Anzio when work to replace its unreliable diesel engine proved problematical; a number of L3 tankettes were used in a similar fashion.

In addition to the tank turrets, ten specially designed armoured revolving hoods (F Pz DT 4007) were installed capable of mounting either an MG34 or MG42. These were constructed from steel plate, but were sufficiently light to be man portable. They could be mounted on either a prepared concrete or wooden shelter or, if necessary, simply on firm ground.

These, and the other tank turrets, were primarily for use against infantry, but a large number of Panther tank turrets were also used as improvised fixed fortifications. They retained their powerful 75mm gun and were often the main anti-tank weapon in the defensive line. The turrets were either taken from production models (Ausf. D and A) or were specially designed for the role. The *Ostwallturm* (or *Ostbefestigung*) as it was known, differed from the standard turret in a number of ways. The cupola was removed and was replaced by a simplified hatch with a rotating periscope, and the roof armour was also increased in thickness because of the greater threat to the turret from artillery fire. The turrets were mounted on either concrete bunkers or, more often, on steel shelters. The Organization Todt had developed a series of prefabricated steel shelters and one of these was adapted to mount a Panther turret. It was constructed in two parts from electrically

| Table 1 – tank turrets installed in Italy | | |
|---|---|---|
| **Type** | **Weapon** | **Number** |
| PzKpfw I | MG34 or MG42 | 91 |
| PzKpfw II | 2cm main gun and MG34 | 17 |
| PzKpfw V 'Panther' | 75mm Kwk 42 L/70 | 48 |
| PzKpfw 38(t) | 3.7cm Kwk 38(t) and MG | 25* |
| Italian M42 | 3.7cm Kwk L/45 | 100* |
| Italian P40 | 7.5cm Kwk L/24 | 100* |
| * Planned | | |

LEFT A destroyed army observation post for a coastal battery (Type 637) that was located on the west coast. In the front section a rangefinder would have been fitted to pinpoint enemy targets for batteries located further to the rear. (US National Archives, 193356)

welded steel plates. The upper box essentially formed the fighting compartment. It held the ammunition for the main weapon and incorporated the turret ball-race onto which the turret was mounted. The lower box was divided into three compartments. The largest formed the living accommodation and was fitted with fold-down bunk beds and a stove. A further room acted as either a general store or as home to various pieces of equipment that provided power for the turret and shelter. And finally, there was a small anteroom fitted with a steel ladder that linked the upper and lower boxes and was also where the main entrance was located. A revetted trench, covered near the entrance, led away from the shelter and linked it to the main trench system at the rear.

A large number of the original steel shelters developed by the Organization Todt were also installed in the various lines to provide protection for troops against enemy artillery and air attack. Other shelters were constructed from timber with soil and rocks heaped on top for added strength. These different shelters were

FOLLOWING PAGE **Nebelwerfer position**
To provide indirect fire support for the various defensive lines the Germans used artillery and mortars but also rocket launchers or *Nebelwerfer* (literally fog throwers). The 15cm *Nebelwerfer* 41 and 21cm *Nebelwerfer* 42 were arguably the best known of these and were encountered on all fronts from 1942 onwards. The distinctive noise of the weapon earned it the sobriquet 'Moaning Minnie' or 'Screaming Mimi'.

The two rocket launchers were broadly the same but the *Nebelwerfer* 42 had five barrels because this offered better balance and stability. The barrels, each 130cm long, were fitted round a central axis and mounted on a two-wheel carriage with a split wheel trail and a front stabilizer plate. Two members of the four-man crew loaded the barrels from the rear. Once loaded the crew retired a safe distance (10m) and the rockets were fired

by electric impulses transmitted along a cable. The *Nebelwerfer* 42 was often employed in specially prepared positions, as depicted here. This was one of six such emplacements in this section of the Hitler Line and was located 1,000m behind the front line. The emplacement consisted of a shelter 6 x 3.3 x 2.2m partly cut into the ridge at the rear and partly built up. Behind the shelter was a 2 x 1.3 x 0.5m concrete block, which was embedded so as to project just 15cm above a hardcore floor. Embedded centrally in the top of the block was a steel ring and towards the back were two further recesses. These accommodated the front stabilizer plate and the two wheels. 3m behind this was a semicircular wall 1.3m high and 1m thick made of hollow bricks (available locally). Ammunition was stored in niches set into the side of the position. These were stacked in specially designed transport cages

*Nebelwerfer position*

An 88mm anti-tank gun pit

The gun was often positioned in specially built open pits to cover key routes. The plate depicts one of these pits in the Gothic Line in late August 1944. The 8.8cm Pak 43 has been dismounted from its limber and sits on its cruciform platform ready for action. Like so many of these positions, however, the defenders have abandoned it after firing only a few shots in anger due to the swift advance of Field Marshal Alexander's armies.

The gun pit was dug to a depth of 60cm so that it provided the crew and the weapon with some protection but at the same time allowed the gun to be fully traversed. To the front of the position bricks were laid flat to provide added protection and to prevent the blast from the muzzle damaging the ground. To either side of the gun ammunition pits were dug. These were 1m square and approximately 0.6–0.8m deep. Further to the rear revetted communication trenches provided the crew with some protection and also led to the crew's shelter (and ultimately to the main trench system). This was 2 x 3 x 1.8m deep and had a roof constructed from timber, which would have been covered in spoil. Further ammunition pits were also provided and could be reached from the rear trench. The position would normally have been covered with camouflage nets but these have been removed ready for action and are piled at the rear of the position, along with the two single-axle limbers that were used to transport the gun.

often linked to fighting positions mounting a variety of weapons including machine guns, mortars, *Nebelwerfer*, artillery pieces and anti-tank guns.

Later in the war there were plans to install tank guns in open pits as improvised anti-tank positions. The powerful 8.8cm guns taken from Jagdpanther tanks were to be fitted to pivot mounts and 5cm 39/1 L60 guns taken from PzKpfw IIIs were to be mounted on makeshift carriages. At the other extreme the Germans built a number of permanent positions. Around the Futa Pass, for example, a number of concrete bunkers to mount anti-tank guns were constructed. On the Adriatic coast near Rimini large coastal emplacements, not dissimilar to those found in the Atlantic Wall, were built. These mounted 15cm guns that had originally been designed for use on ships. Dragon's teeth, or *Höckerhindernisse*, which had first been employed by the Germans in the West Wall, were also used extensively around the coast in attempt to deter a further Allied amphibious assault. These were essentially reinforced concrete pyramids poured in rows and designed to either stop an enemy tank completely or to expose the thinner armour of the underside of the tank to the defenders' anti-tank guns.

RIGHT One of the 15cm naval guns in its concrete emplacement. Four of these positions were constructed in the vicinity of Rimini to protect against a potential amphibious assault. The New Zealanders captured them during their drive along the coast in September 1944. (Imperial War Museum, NA 18992)

# The living site

The title of this section is something of a misnomer because in contrast to the major defensive positions of World War II, like the Maginot Line, the majority of the defences constructed by the Germans in Italy were not permanent defences. They were fieldworks, or *Feldmäßig*, and were only designed for short-term occupation. The term *Feldmäßig* is also somewhat misleading because although many of the positions were simply revetted earthworks a large number were built using prefabricated steel shelters or were constructed from reinforced concrete.

Nevertheless it is possible to provide a 'human angle' to the story of the German defences in Italy both in terms of those individuals who built the defences and those who manned them. Responsibility for reconnoitring possible positions for the defences and what type of fortification should go where was the domain of the army engineers. These specialists were trained for this role and could draw on a wealth of experience from the digging of the trench systems in World War I, through the building of the West Wall and later still the Atlantic Wall, and increasingly the experiences on the Eastern Front.

Although army engineers provided the technical input the actual construction work was the responsibility of the Organization Todt (OT). This was a paramilitary organization created in 1933 under Dr Fritz Todt and was established to carry out major public works programmes, principally the construction of the *Autobahnen*. Later the organization was tasked with building the West Wall, which ran along Germany's western border, and later still the Atlantic Wall. In Italy the Organization Todt acted as overseer of an army of labourers made up of a mixture of locally recruited and foreign workers. Some of the workers volunteered, others were enticed by the prospect of better conditions, but most were simply impressed.

LEFT This field position near Monghidoro formed part of the Gothic Line and was captured by US forces before it could be completed. The trench leading to the dugout is visible at the rear as are the ammunition niches. The pedestal in the middle might have mounted a small anti-tank or anti-aircraft gun. (Imperial War Museum, NA19207)

The majority of the workers who were press-ganged were local Italians, but workers were also drafted from another source in Italy. Until very recently Italy had been one of the main Axis powers and a number of Italian divisions remained loyal to the fascist cause. They were trained in Germany and fought alongside their former ally. The men who volunteered to serve in these units were vetted by the Organization Todt, which selected those individuals with special skills to serve with the labour battalions. Later in the war many of the soldiers serving with the Italian divisions started to transfer to the OT because of the promise of better rations and greater security.

Of the foreign workers employed in Italy many were prisoners of war from the Eastern Front, especially former Red Army soldiers captured following the invasion of the Soviet Union in 1941. These men were kept in POW camps where the conditions were extremely harsh and many 'volunteered' to serve in the labour battalions where conditions were slightly more bearable. The very nature of this work – outside and often in remote areas – also offered more opportunities to abscond and a number of POWs escaped and fought with the Italian partisans. As the Allies liberated areas of Italy many gave themselves up to the British and American authorities and at the end of the war they were repatriated to the Soviet Union. Here they faced an uncertain future, because they were viewed as cowards or collaborators or both, in spite of the fact that they had served with the Red Army and had later escaped to fight the Germans in Italy.

With perhaps the exception of genuine volunteers, most of the labourers who worked on the defences lacked motivation; they often worked slowly and sometimes work was deliberately sabotaged. But of far greater importance in terms of the quality, quantity and preparedness of the defences were the shortages of raw materials. The aptly named Operation *Strangle*, which saw Allied bombers target communication links in northern Italy, had reduced the flow of materials to a trickle and this brought with it a further problem. If Kesselring's forces were to fight a successful delaying action in Italy then it was vital that the fighting strength of his units be maintained. To do this he required regular reinforcements from Germany and therefore manpower had to be released from fortification work to repair roads, bridges and rail links.

Of equal concern were direct air attacks on construction sites. By this stage in the war the Allies had complete air superiority and could observe and strike at enemy targets with impunity. As a consequence much of the construction work had to be carried out under the cover of darkness and during the day building sites had to be heavily camouflaged. Some positions were even constructed inside buildings to avoid detection, with the outer shell being demolished later as the enemy approached.

The Allied bombing, a less than committed workforce and, later, partisan activity undoubtedly made an already challenging building programme even more difficult. True, the defences constructed by the Germans were

BELOW A flight of steps constructed from logs held in place by wooden pegs. They led to a German position in the Gothic Line. Camouflage nets, that would have prevented Allied planes spotting the position, hang limply at the side. (US National Archives, 359053)

not on the scale of the Maginot Line or the West Wall and were often little more than simple fieldworks. Nevertheless, they still required an enormous amount of time, men and materials to complete.

The installation of the *MG Panzernest* is a good case in point. Firstly, the armoured crab had to be transported to its final location. This was a difficult and lengthy task in itself because the nest weighed over a tonne and could only be moved at a sedate 10kph. Meantime, the installation crew of 12 (one officer and 11 men) had to dig the hole into which the shelter would be positioned. The excavation had to be dug in the shape of the nest approximately 2.2m long, 2m wide and 1.2m deep, which was not easy when the ground was baked hard, frozen solid or waterlogged.

Once the crab had been delivered it was positioned so that it could be lowered into the pre-prepared hole. Further digging was now required under the nest and the wheels so that the turret eventually rested on its top and the wheels could be removed. Next the tow bar and axle were removed and either returned for use with another nest or carefully stored nearby. The loose fittings inside were removed, the hatch was closed and final checks made before the nest was rotated through 180 degrees and dropped into its hole.

Three men using wooden heavers lifted the heavy nose section while the other men secured a rope to the base and pulled. Once the centre of gravity had been reached the nest would fall unceremoniously into its final resting place. If the nest was not pointing in the right direction, crowbars could be inserted in the axle holes and ropes attached so that the team could pull the nest round. With the nest in place stones or timbers were packed into place to protect the thinner lower section of the crab. The axle holes were sealed and the whole covered in earth and camouflaged. Finally, the MG34 could be fitted and the necessary vertical and horizontal alignment completed.

The installation of the Panther turrets on OT steel shelters was equally onerous, but on a much larger scale. Firstly, the position of the turret had to be agreed, which was dictated by tactical considerations and by ground conditions. The turret had to be positioned on slightly rising ground, so that it did not stand out against the horizon, and away from prominent landmarks, like road junctions, even if this meant that in some cases the turret did not have all-round operation. It was also important to consider the underground water level because any flooding would seriously jeopardize the operation of the turret – the motor and electrical equipment were below ground level.

Once the location of the turret had been decided it was the responsibility of the Organization Todt to transport the upper and lower boxes and to install them

LEFT One of the numerous *MG Panzernester*, or 'crabs', used in the Hitler Line. This example was captured before it could be buried in the ground. Still attached at the front is the limber and a shattered wheel. The whole structure would have been towed upside down. (Imperial War Museum, NA15778)

(although in reality the crew was often required to help). The two base sections were transported to Italy by rail and from the station they were loaded onto specially designed trailers that were then towed by tractors to the final site for installation. However, by this stage in the war tractors were scarce and fuel even more so, and so to ease the transport problems it was decided that wherever possible the turrets were to be installed as near as possible to the rail terminus or at least near good roads a short distance away. The difficulties with moving the shelters meant that increasingly the OT had to rely on Army Groups to provide help. In the construction of the Green Line in Fourteenth Army's zone Pz.Berge-Kp.9 (9th Panzer Recovery Company) was responsible for transporting the Panther turrets from the railway station to their final destination. And Italian civilians interviewed later also reported instances of oxen being used to tow the trailers.

At the chosen site a hole was excavated that was deep and wide enough to accommodate both steel boxes and the collar of reinforced concrete 1–1.5m thick. At the bottom of the excavation a concrete base was laid to ensure that everything was level. A mobile crane then lowered the base unit onto this. The upper section was similarly unloaded and fitted on top. Once complete the concrete jacket was poured and when this had set the spoil could be backfilled and the approach to the entrance completed, which included a soakaway to prevent flooding. However, just as was the case with the tractors, as Germany's situation deteriorated heavy lifting gear was increasingly difficult to find. Instead the workers had to manoeuvre the individual sections along 'rail tracks' to their final resting place. It was then necessary to dig an incline down which the boxes were lowered. Once in place the concrete could be poured and the soil backfilled.

And work did not finish there. Because the turret sat so close to the ground it was essential that nothing prevented it from rotating and that it had a clear field of fire. The crew was therefore required to remove plants and trees (and in the winter snow) that might otherwise impair the effective operation of the turret. At the same time it was vital that the structure was heavily camouflaged, which meant erecting a framework for camouflage netting, or matting and digging a sandbag-lined channel into which the gun barrel was depressed to eliminate the telltale shadow.

Once the various defensive positions had been completed they were ready for occupation, although this would only normally happen when the enemy

RIGHT A Panther turret and steel shelter ready for installation. In the foreground are the rails on which the lower box, which formed the crew's living quarters, was moved into place. The two sections have been covered in hay in an effort to camouflage them. (Imperial War Museum, NA18343)

LEFT A Panther turret gun barrel showing the sandbag channel that it was lowered into to either hide its distinctive shadow from aerial observation or to reduce the strain on the elevating gear. (Imperial War Museum, HU60080)

was pressing. A crew of two operating a standard MG34 machine gun manned the *MG Panzernest*. When the machine gun was in operation it generated exhaust fumes and dust that needed to be extracted.[15] This was achieved through a foot-operated fan that needed to be fully depressed 60–70 times a minute to clear the powder gases. Two treadles were included so that both members of the crew could operate it. The shelter was also fitted with a stove that provided a valuable source of heat. But in spite of these concessions to human comfort, conditions inside were not pleasant when the position was in action and it was also very cramped. The *MG Panzernest* did, however, provide the crew with valuable protection, both against the weather and enemy fire; the shelter being proof against any weapon up to 4.7cm in calibre.

A specially trained crew of three – commander, gunner and loader – manned the Panther turrets. These men operated the turret in much the same way as a standard production-model tank. However, the turret was not fitted with power traverse, which meant that the gunner, assisted by the loader, had to rotate the turret by hand, which, because of the high gearing, was extremely slow. The turret was fitted with a fan that ensured noxious fumes were vented outside, and a compressed-air system that was used to clear the gun barrel.

When not in action the crew would eat and sleep in the lower box. This was fitted with a stove and there were up to nine bunk beds (six if a radio was fitted), which meant that other troops could also be accommodated if necessary. A hand-operated fan was fitted to provide fresh air.

The men who manned these turrets formed part of a *Festungs (Panther-Turm) Kompanie* normally made up of 12 turrets. In April 1944, Tenth Army established

---

[15] The MG42 could not be fitted in the *MG Panzernest* because it generated too many fumes for the fan to cope with, although a new more powerful fan was being developed.

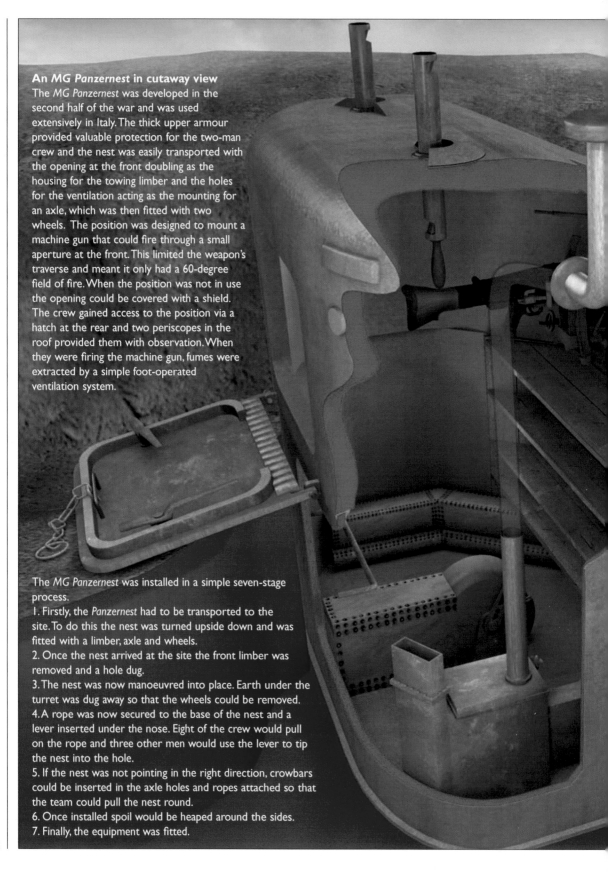

### An *MG Panzernest* in cutaway view

The *MG Panzernest* was developed in the second half of the war and was used extensively in Italy. The thick upper armour provided valuable protection for the two-man crew and the nest was easily transported with the opening at the front doubling as the housing for the towing limber and the holes for the ventilation acting as the mounting for an axle, which was then fitted with two wheels. The position was designed to mount a machine gun that could fire through a small aperture at the front. This limited the weapon's traverse and meant it only had a 60-degree field of fire. When the position was not in use the opening could be covered with a shield. The crew gained access to the position via a hatch at the rear and two periscopes in the roof provided them with observation. When they were firing the machine gun, fumes were extracted by a simple foot-operated ventilation system.

The *MG Panzernest* was installed in a simple seven-stage process.

1. Firstly, the *Panzernest* had to be transported to the site. To do this the nest was turned upside down and was fitted with a limber, axle and wheels.
2. Once the nest arrived at the site the front limber was removed and a hole dug.
3. The nest was now manoeuvred into place. Earth under the turret was dug away so that the wheels could be removed.
4. A rope was now secured to the base of the nest and a lever inserted under the nose. Eight of the crew would pull on the rope and three other men would use the lever to tip the nest into the hole.
5. If the nest was not pointing in the right direction, crowbars could be inserted in the axle holes and ropes attached so that the team could pull the nest round.
6. Once installed spoil would be heaped around the sides.
7. Finally, the equipment was fitted.

a Panther turret company to man the positions on the Hitler Line. This was attached to 15th Panzergrenadier Division, which initially held the Liri Valley, and when this division was relieved Kampfgruppe Straffner absorbed the Panther turret company. 1st Fallschirmjäger Division manned other turrets along the line, particularly around Piedimonte in the shadow of Monte Cassino. After the battle one of the men of this division, Gefreiter Fries, was awarded the Knight's Cross for his part in destroying a number of Allied tanks. The turrets manned by crews from 15th Panzergrenadier Division were seemingly not as fortunate as their comrades as many were killed during the battle.

The Panther turret company that manned the turrets on the Hitler Line was later reformed under Tenth Army and given the designation Festungs (Panther-Turm) Kp.1. This unit manned the Panther turrets at the eastern end of the Green Line. A sister unit, Festungs (Panther-Turm) Kp.2, was established by Fourteenth Army in July 1944 to man positions in the west and to cover the central passes. Later in the war the organization of Panther turret crews became more ordered so that in addition to these two companies, Festungs (Panther-Turm) Kp. 1209 and 1210 were formed. By the beginning of April 1945, all of these units were stationed in the Voralpenstellung in north-eastern Italy.

More normally the defensive positions were manned by ordinary artillerymen, grenadiers, infantrymen or quasi infantry like the *Fallschirmjäger* who since the successful, but costly, landing on Crete had been used as ground troops rather than as an airborne assault force. With relatively few exceptions – some of the larger permanent defences and the Panther turrets being good examples – the unit manning the position was responsible for providing the weaponry whether it be an artillery, anti-tank or anti-aircraft gun, a mortar, a *Nebelwerfer* or simply a machine gun.

Often the fighting positions were linked to OT steel shelters or dugouts. These provided the troops with protection against the elements and somewhere to eat and sleep. They were often fitted with bunk beds and a stove for warmth and to cook on. More importantly they also provided a safe haven against enemy fire. Once the enemy barrage and air attacks had subsided the defenders would emerge from their subterranean refuge and man their weapons.

This was especially true of the paratroopers defending Monte Cassino. Work on the Gustav Line had begun during the autumn of 1943 and eventually some 44,000 men, under the direction of Engineer General Bessell, were set to work on this position. They included army construction units, Organization Todt

RIGHT An excavation ready to accommodate the upper and lower boxes for a Panther turret. The base section would have been manoeuvred down the inclined plane, a technique used when no lifting gear was available. (J. Plowman)

personnel, Italian auxiliaries and labour battalions. The latter would sometimes be hired in exchange for food or tobacco, which after four years of war were in short supply, or German soldiers simply rounded men up at the point of a gun and forced them to work.

In mid-November 1943, plans were instituted for a switch line behind the Cassino position. This was named after the Führer and was to be of 'fortress strength', which essentially meant it was to be built using concrete and steel emplacements. Once again the Organization Todt oversaw the construction work, but the new defences required additional manpower and the workforce was supplemented with the addition of Slovak and Russian labour battalions. However, shortages of materials, exacerbated by variable standards of work and differences of opinion between military engineers and Todt technicians, meant that work had still not been completed by early May, and so

ABOVE An Allied soldier descends steps from a German machine-gun position that formed part of the Gothic Line. To the right is a shelter dug into the side of the slope with the walls strengthened with timber and brushwood. (Imperial War Museum, NA18334)

units manning the defences had to complete the final preparations, including laying mines.

As early as December 1943, consideration had been given to a 'C' position that was to run from the coast south of Rome to the Adriatic. Engineer General Bessell was again tasked with reconnoitring the position, but work did not commence immediately because priority had to be given to construction of the Gustav and Hitler lines. However, the requirement for a defensive line to protect the Italian capital was given added urgency by the Allied landings at Anzio in January 1944 and soon after work began on the Caesar Line. Progress was unspectacular and at the beginning of March Kesselring ordered work on the defences be expedited and that the line should be finished by the end of April.

Engineer Major General Eric Rothe, who in March 1944 had been briefly in charge of work on the Hitler Line, was given responsibility for overseeing the work. Under him was the usual hodgepodge of military and paramilitary staff and a relatively small number of local labourers and workers from the east. To meet Kesselring's target an attempt was made to accelerate construction work on the line by impressing more local labourers, but it was increasingly difficult to find able-bodied men as many had fled their homes to avoid just such an eventuality. Not only that, there was a desperate need for manpower to repair bomb-damaged roads and Rothe and his staff were later withdrawn from work on the Caesar Line to coordinate this work.

Resources were also increasingly concentrated on the Green Line, work on which had resumed in earnest in June 1944. Initially this was the responsibility of the Rear Army Command, known as Armeeabteilung von Zangen. To carry out this task General von Zangen had under his command engineers, members of the OT and thousands of Italian labourers supported by technicians from Scandinavia and Eastern Europe.

At the beginning of July Tenth and Fourteenth Armies assumed responsibility for their respective sections of the line and von Zangen's group reverted to corps status. On reviewing the defences they had inherited von Vietinghoff and Lemelsen were less than impressed. Their respective reactions to the parlous state of the defences, however, were in marked contrast. Lemelsen concentrated his energies on the situation at the front rather than the completion of the Green Line. Von Vietinghoff was almost the complete opposite. He had already secured the services of Engineer General Bessell, who was to work strengthening the defences along the Adriatic seaboard, which potentially offered the Allies the greatest opportunity for a breakthrough. Von Vietinghoff also ensured that

RIGHT A view from one of the many concrete emplacements constructed around the Futa Pass that were captured by 91st (US) Infantry Division. This anti-tank emplacement had a clear field of fire across the tank trap in the middle distance and the road further on. (Imperial War Museum, NA18929)

BELOW A number of bunkers were built on the Lido di Venezia, a strip of land that separates the Venetian Lagoon from the Adriatic Sea. This covered emplacement would have housed a large-calibre naval gun. (B. Lowry)

his corps and divisions, who had their own headquarters construction personnel in the Green Line, worked in close cooperation with Staff Bessell to ensure that their battle experience was used to advantage.

In fairness to von Zangen and his staff, construction of the Green Line was not their sole responsibility; they were also in charge of security of the rear areas. Moreover, their efforts to construct the defences had been beset by shortages of labour and of materials and they had also had to contend with intense partisan action. Once the army took charge the situation improved and

good progress was made on the defences. That is not to say that there were no further problems. The work on Green I suffered from the diversion of skilled engineer units to supervise the repair of the railways and bridges and the construction of temporary ferries over the Po. Men and materials were also diverted to the coastal defences to protect against a possible landing around Rimini or on the Venice–Trieste coast.

Indeed, resources were so stretched it was all they could do to concentrate on Green I; no work had even been started on Green II. On 12 August von Vietinghoff directed Bessell to plan the move of his staff and the bulk of his engineers to Green II by 1 September, leaving the rest to strengthen the vulnerable sectors in Green I. But these orders were overtaken by events because by that time the Allies were already through Green I and were threatening the reserve position. Fortunately for von Vietinghoff, although no work on this position had been completed it was naturally strong and was defended by fresh units. This provided Tenth Army with valuable breathing space and the bulk of the army engineer battalions in the Green Line, as well as the various labour units, were able to retire in good order. They were placed under the command of LXXVI Panzer Corps and were set to work on defences to the rear, including the Rimini Line, where a further 10,000 labourers were rounded up to press ahead with construction work.

At the end of August a decision had also been taken to accelerate work on the Voralpenstellung, which drained off further engineers and construction workers from Green I. These defences, and those of the Venetian Line, were being constructed under the direction of General Buelowius, the Inspector of Land Fortifications South West. Under his command he had somewhere in the region of 5,000 German fortification specialists and a significant number of impressed Italian workers under the Organization Todt. However, as the war drew to a close workers on these defences melted away and many of the planned fortifications were not started or were incomplete.

LEFT A section of German trench that was hewn out of solid rock. The trench formed part of the Gothic Line defences and dominated a hairpin bend in the Apennines. US forces captured it in 1944. (US National Archives, 198878)

# Operational history

## Sicily

On 10 July 1943, the Allies landed on Sicily in what was the largest amphibious assault in Europe up to that point. This was a multinational force under the command of Field Marshal Alexander. Montgomery's Eighth Army landed on the east coast and experienced little opposition and, as hoped, the naval base of Syracuse was captured on the first day. Patton's Seventh Army landed in the south-west of the island where the beaches were more heavily fortified and where resistance was stiffer. Nevertheless, by 12 July the beachhead had been secured and the Germans and Italians were on the defensive.

The Eighth Army made the main thrust of the Allied attack with the Americans securing the flank. But Alexander's strategy meant that the chance of splitting the island and isolating part of the enemys' forces in the west was lost. The Axis forces, under the command of General Hube, fell back to the first of their defensive lines, the Etna Line. This held firm against a four-pronged attack by Montgomery and allowed 15th Panzergrenadier Division to the west to fall back in good order and to dig in around Troina in the knowledge that its line of retreat was secure. Hube's forces were now ensconced in a line that ran from Acireale to San Fratello. The British continued to press from the south while the Americans pushed east. The 1st (US) Infantry Division fought a fierce five-day battle to dislodge German troops from Troina and further north 'Along the entire face of the San Fratello ridge, pillboxes, trenches and gun emplacements made things tough for the 3rd Division.'[16] However, pressure from the Americans and the British eventually forced the Germans to withdraw and plans for a total evacuation were prepared. A series of defensive lines were established further back, each shorter than the last and requiring fewer troops to defend so allowing the rest to be evacuated. The Axis forces surrendered on 17 August, but by that point 40,000 German and 62,000 Italian troops with much of their equipment had been safely transported to the mainland.

## Gustav Line

A little over a fortnight later the Allies landed on the Italian mainland and, after an initial scare at Salerno, consolidated their hold and advanced north to the so-called Winter Line. The Allies hoped to bounce this position before the enemy had time to settle in. To the north of Monte Cassino the French Expeditionary Corps (FEC) attacked towards Atina. They successfully negotiated the perils of the Rapido River and closed on the outworks of the Gustav Line proper, but tired and cold from their exertions in the depths of a bitter Italian winter and meeting stiff German resistance the attack was suspended.

General Clark, who now commanded American forces in Italy, had argued that attacks be launched on both flanks of the Gustav Line to increase the chances of a breakthrough and on 20 January II (US) Corps began what was hoped would be the decisive thrust across the Rapido and up the Liri Valley. General Walker's 36th (US) Infantry Division was

BELOW An observation post constructed by the Italians located south-east of Itri. The position was absorbed into the defences of the Winter Line. It was camouflaged to resemble natural rock and blend in with the surroundings. (TM30-246 *Tactical Interpretation of Air Photos 1954*, Figure 852)

[16]Garland and H. McGaw Smyth, *Sicily and the Surrender of Italy* (Center of Military History, Washington, 1986), p.353.

ordered to lead the attack. Covered by an artillery barrage the Texans advanced to the river with their assault boats and made their way across, but were met with a hail of machine-gun fire. The defenders, men of 15th Panzergrenadier Division, had sheltered in deep dugouts during the barrage and now emerged to man their weapons in pre-prepared positions, which had been carefully sited to create a belt of interlocking fire.

Having reached the far bank there was no respite for the Americans. Mines and barbed wire blocked their advance and, trapped in their tiny bridgehead with no easy route to retreat, they were subjected to intense mortar, artillery and *Nebelwerfer* fire that had been pre-registered on both banks. Eventually it was realized that the position was untenable. A few men managed to extricate themselves, but the rest were either killed or captured.

Still reeling from the bloody reverse crossing the Rapido, Clark tried to regain the initiative by launching another attack north of Cassino on the night of 24/25 January. General Ryder's 34th (US) Infantry Division, supported by the FEC, was to cross the Rapido and, having secured a bridgehead, capture Monte Cassino. The defences in this section of the line were particularly strong and made any advance extremely difficult. The regimental commander of 133rd Infantry Regiment wrote, 'MG nests in steel and concrete bunkers had to be stormed. Progress was measured by yards and by buildings. Each building had been converted into an enemy strongpoint … Casualties were heavy.'[17] Not surprisingly the Americans struggled to make any headway, and with no armoured support the attack faltered. A better crossing point was identified and a renewed attack proved more fruitful with tanks able to support the infantry. They were 'hampered by narrow streets and poor fields of fire, but on several occasions were able to destroy enemy strongpoints in buildings with point blank fire.'[18] The signs looked promising and Clark signalled Alexander that Monte Cassino would fall soon and von Senger und Etterlin, the commander of XIV Panzer Corps, suggested to Kesselring that German forces retire to the Caesar Line.

Victory seemed to be in sight and one more thrust was ordered on 11 February. But this proved to be ill conceived. The Americans had suffered terrible casualties and morale was low. Ryder's division was simply not capable of delivering the *coup de grace*. The first battle of Monte Cassino had ended and the Gustav Line had held firm.

The Americans were relieved by elements of 4th Indian Division, who were now tasked with capturing Monastery Hill. Meanwhile 2nd New Zealand Division was ordered to capture Cassino railway station. On 15 February the operation was launched but both attacks were unsuccessful. However, the second battle for Monte Cassino is most noteworthy for the decision to bomb the abbey atop the hill which the Allies believed was occupied by the Germans. It later transpired that this was not the case, but the Germans were not slow to seize the opportunity and integrate the ruins into their defences.

A massive aerial and artillery bombardment similarly preceded the Third Battle for Monte Cassino, which it was hoped would smash the enemy defences and allow the Indians and New Zealanders to achieve their respective goals. On the morning of 15 March the bombardment began. The results looked impressive and indeed the defenders in the town and on the surrounding hills suffered terrible losses, but enough survived in deep dugouts and caves hewn into the solid rock to man basement strongpoints and other positions. At the same time the bombardment served to flatten most of the buildings still standing, making navigation difficult and ensuring it was all but impossible for the armour to support the infantry. Where the tanks did get forward the Germans easily picked them off using hand-held anti-tank weapons or mines. The New Zealand infantry did manage to reach Highway

---

[17] J. Ellis, *Cassino. The Hollow Victory: The Battle For Rome January–June 1944* (Andre Deutsch, London, 1984), p.127.
[18] Ibid., p.127.

ABOVE A US soldier examines the internal workings of a captured *MG Panzernest*. It has been covered in rocks for added protection and camouflage. Just visible in the right foreground is a German mess tin. (US National Archives, 187023)

6 and eventually some tanks did worm their way forward and engage enemy strongpoints. One of which was centred on the Continental Hotel, which dominated Route 6. A tank had been built into the entrance hall and it was key in preventing the New Zealanders pushing armour down the road to Rome. By 23 March both sides were exhausted and the New Zealanders' attack was called off. Meanwhile, the Indians had captured Castle Hill and Hangman's Hill, but their hold was not sufficiently strong to act as a springboard for an attack on the monastery and they simply dug in to consolidate their gains. Eighth Army now reorganized and prepared for a new attack in the spring in what was hoped would be the final breakthrough.

The Allies had tried to breach the Gustav Line on three occasions and although success had been tantalizingly close on a number of occasions the Germans held firm. This was partly because of the natural strength of the position with its fast-flowing rivers and mountains that dominated the main routes of advance. In part it was due to poor Allied leadership. The decision to bomb the Monastery gave the defenders an ideal defensive battleground and made combined operations almost impossible for attacking units. Crucially, the great opportunity of outflanking the position with the amphibious assault at Anzio was squandered by overly conservative commanders on the ground whose inaction was summed up by Churchill when he told the Chiefs-of-Staff, 'We hoped to land a wild cat that would tear out the bowels of the Boche. Instead we have stranded a vast whale with its tail flopping about in the water!'[19] But the defences undoubtedly played a part in blunting the Allied attacks. The defences provided valuable protection against the Allied air and artillery bombardment and the strongpoints, carefully sited so that they could bring devastating fire to bear on the enemy, proved to be exceptionally difficult to neutralize. Eventually the Gustav Line was breached and the Eighth Army advanced along the Liri Valley, but it was now faced with the prospect of defeating the Hitler Line.

## Hitler Line

At first light on 19 May a probing attack was launched against the Hitler Line. Two battalions of infantry supported by tanks of 17th/21st Lancers and the Ontario Regiment of Canada advanced towards Aquino. Screened by early morning mist the composite force made good progress, but the fog cleared and 'At that moment a well camouflaged high velocity anti-tank gun, in a steel and concrete pillbox, [an emplaced Panther turret] opened fire at point blank range from the right, holed all three tanks at least twice and set them on fire.'[20] The tanks of the Ontario Regiment engaged the enemy, but it was an uneven struggle and under the cover of darkness those tanks that could withdraw did so. All of the tanks in the two leading squadrons suffered at least one direct hit and in total the Ontario's lost 13 tanks.

Another probing attack was put in against the defences around Pontecorvo on 22 May by 48th Highlanders of Canada and a squadron of tanks from 142nd Royal Armoured Corps (the Suffolks). The result was much the same with three of the Suffolks' tanks knocked out by an emplaced Panther turret. All efforts were now concentrated on the main attack planned for the following day, which was to be made by 1st Canadian Infantry Division supported by 25th Tank Brigade.

[19] M. Gilbert, *Winston Churchill 1874–1965, Vol. VII, 1941–1945* (Heinemann: London, 1986), p.667
[20] CNA, RG24 Vol.1920 *Operations of the 1st Canadian Armoured Brigade in Italy May 1944 to February 1945.*

The main thrust was to be delivered by two battalions of 2nd Canadian Infantry Brigade – the Seaforth Highlanders on the left supported by two squadrons of tanks of the North Irish Horse and the Princess Patricia's Canadian Light Infantry on the right supported by a single squadron. At the same time the 48th Highlanders were to maintain the pressure on the enemy around Pontecorvo and, on their right, 3rd Infantry Brigade, supported by 51st Royal Tank Regiment, was to launch a feint to keep the enemy guessing as to the Allies' true intentions.

Somewhat unexpectedly these secondary operations enjoyed a certain amount of success with the tanks of the 142nd RAC destroying an emplaced Panther turret protecting Pontecorvo and 51st RTR advancing to the Aquino–Pontecorvo road – the first objective of the main thrust – and in so doing also put a Panther turret out of action. However, the main attack of 2nd Infantry Brigade was not going as well.

The Patricias reached the enemy wire, but their supporting tanks were stopped by an undetected minefield and as they struggled to find a way through four of their number were picked off by enemy anti-tank guns and the remainder fell back to find another way forward. Unaware of their compatriots' difficulties the Loyal Edmontons, supported by a squadron of 51st RTR, followed the Patricias in accordance with the second phase of the attack. The tanks, however, were similarly balked by mines and a number fell victim to the Panther turrets and their supporting anti-tank guns.

To their left the Seaforth Highlanders and the North Irish Horse made better progress, but when only 100m from their first objective the tanks came under heavy anti-tank fire, which accounted for five of their number including the squadron leader. The remainder beat a hasty retreat and, together with tanks from C squadron that had been held in reserve, advanced on a new axis. This force accounted for another Panther turret, but lost seven tanks in the process.

In spite of the losses the unremitting pressure along the southern portion of the line had forced the enemy to retreat. The attack against Aquino was now resumed to exploit the enemy's disarray. Men of the Lancashire Fusiliers supported by two troops of tanks of 14th Canadian Armoured Regiment advanced on the town, but soon four of the six tanks had been destroyed and the others retired. Despite being outflanked it was clear that the enemy still held the defences in strength and it was not until the following day that the enemy finally withdrew, having first demolished the two Panther turrets defending the town.

In total 25th Tank Brigade lost 44 tanks (although some were later recovered); the heaviest tank losses inflicted on the Eighth Army in the Italian campaign. An intelligence report written after the battle noted, 'In front of each position there was a graveyard of Churchills and some Shermans ... This is, at present, the price of reducing a Panther turret and it would seem to be an excellent investment for Hitler.'[21]

## Caesar Line

At the same time as Leese's Eighth Army launched its attack to breach the Hitler Line, Alexander ordered Clark's Fifth Army to break out of the Anzio bridgehead. Truscott, the commander of VI (US) Corps at Anzio planned to attack towards Cisterna and then advance to Valmontone with a view to cutting Route 6, one of von Vietinghoff's (AOK 10) main lines of retreat. This plan

BELOW A Panther turret positioned near Aquino in the Hitler Line. The German defenders demolished the turret before it fell into Allied hands. The photograph clearly shows the metre-thick collar that protected the upper and lower armoured boxes. The entranceway and revetted trench are just visible in the foreground. (Public Record Office, WO291/1315)

[21] G. Nicholson, *The Canadians in Italy, Vol. II, Official History of the Canadian Army in the Second World War* (Queen's Printer: Ottawa, 1956), p.396.

was endorsed by Alexander and initially VI (US) Corps made good progress towards it objective. However, on 25 May Clark changed the focus of the attack away from Valmontone towards Rome. This change of tack undoubtedly had a number of military advantages, but it was also fraught with danger because it would involve attacking the strongest section of the Caesar Line, which was held by General Schlemm's very strong and highly motivated I Fallschirmjäger Corps, which was more than capable of defeating any such attack.

Only 3rd (US) Infantry Division continued its advance towards Valmontone. The Old Ironsides, 1st (US) Armored Division, which had been guarding its left flank, was now ordered to head north as were 34th and 45th (US) Infantry Divisions, which were tasked with capturing Lanuvio and Campoleone respectively. The new operation was launched on 26 May, but almost immediately the attack of 1st (US) Armored Division was stopped dead by mines and well-placed anti-tank guns manned by 4th Fallschirmjäger Division. The advance of 34th (US) Infantry Division was similarly halted on 27 May and slightly later 45th (US) Infantry Division experienced the same fate. The assault on the Caesar Line was resumed on 29 May with an attack by 1st (US) Armored Division slightly further to the west, but this was also unsuccessful. As soon as the tanks approached the defences they were engaged by anti-tank guns and infantry armed with *Panzerfaust* hand-held anti-tank weapons. By dusk 37 American tanks had been knocked out, most of them destroyed. A further attempt to breach the line was launched the following day, this time with infantry in the lead, but the result was the same.

General Walker's 36th (US) Infantry Division had replaced 1st (US) Armored Division in the line after it had initially been withdrawn and it was envisaged that the infantrymen would launch another set-piece attack against the main defences of the Caesar Line. But General Walker, whose men had suffered heavy casualties by adopting such tactics at Salerno and, more recently, crossing the Rapido, was not keen and considered a number of alternatives. One that presented itself was to attack through the Alban Hills rather than going round. The OKW had largely ignored the hills, in part because they lay on the corps boundary, and in part because they were considered unsuitable for an enemy attack. A patrol ordered to reconnoitre enemy dispositions on Monte Artemisio found that it had not been fortified and nor was it occupied. But equally there were no obvious routes to the top save for a narrow farm track. However, engineers were convinced that the track could be widened to take military vehicles and so the decision was taken to attack on 30 May. Two

RIGHT An Italian armoured pillbox, possible a navy observation post, captured by the Americans at Anzio in 1944. The structure was constructed from steel plate and was accessed by a door at the rear. The apertures, which provided all-round observation, could be closed if necessary. (US National Archives, 208N 22340)

infantry regiments made their way to the top of the mountain under the cover of darkness. They caught the small garrison completely by surprise and captured it without a shot being fired. Engineers soon set to work improving the track and men of Walker's division dug in on the heights. Through a mixture of complacency and élan the 36th (US) Infantry Division had captured the 1,000m peak. In so doing the Caesar Line had been turned and, on 5 June, Mark Clark was in Rome.

# Gothic Line

Clark's decision to attack the strongest portion of the Caesar Line not only allowed the Germans to extricate themselves from a possible encirclement, but also meant he unnecessarily weakened his divisions, which made it difficult for them to pursue the enemy north of Rome. This, together with the panoply of lines and defensive positions that the Germans had established between Rome and the Gothic Line, slowed the Allied advance. The Eternal City fell on 5 June but it was not until the end of August that the Allies were in a position to launch an attack against the last bastion before the Alps.

Although it was clear that the Allies would soon launch a new offensive, when it started on the night of 25/26 August it came as a complete surprise to Kesselring and von Vietinghoff, the commander of Tenth Army. They had been considering the possible withdrawal to the Po, Operation *Herbstnebel*, while the movement of divisions in and out of the line distracted their immediate subordinates. At the same time, divisional commanders were preoccupied with the phased withdrawal of troops from their forward positions into the Green Line proper; the tardy withdrawal in part driven by Hitler's insistence that no ground should be given up to the enemy. The result was that many of the troops had no time to familiarize themselves with the defences they were supposed to be manning. Not that all the positions were complete; a large number of Panther turrets had still to be installed in the ground and signs were still in place detailing safe lanes through the minefields.

With the Germans taken by surprise, Eighth Army, in the first phase of the battle, smashed through the defences of Green I with unexpected ease. Their advance was also facilitated by the devastating effect of bombing and strafing by the Desert Air Force. When 26th Panzer Division was committed to the battle on 28 August it found that 'air and artillery bombardment had already obliterated many of the positions they should have occupied'.[22] And minefields that had taken a considerable time to lay were 'simply lifted from the air'.[23]

The air and artillery bombardment also served to unnerve the enemy. When 2nd Canadian Infantry Brigade and their supporting tanks from 21st Tank Brigade launched their attack on Monteluro on 1 September they 'found the intricate and deep system of trenches, MG posts and anti-tank gun positions abandoned.'[24] Elsewhere, the enemy was more stubborn and was only dislodged by small unit actions and individual bravery. In fighting on the previous day 46th Division captured Montegridolfo, Mondaino and Pt 374, the highest point along the ridge half way between the two villages. An achievement that was made possible by the 'brilliantly successful attack of 1st/4th Hampshires in which Lieutenant G.R. Norton won the VC for dealing with three German concrete weapon emplacements.'[25]

Once through Green I the Allies should have been faced with the equally daunting prospect of breaching

BELOW Allied infantrymen advance past a captured *MG Panzernest* in the Gothic Line in September 1944. The aperture through which the machine gun was fired is just visible as is the metal shutter that could be secured across the opening. (Imperial War Museum, NA18172)

[22] W. Jackson, *The Mediterranean and Middle East, Vol. VI, Victory in the Mediterranean, Part II, June to October 1944* (HMSO, London, 1987), p.245.
[23] Ibid., p.242.
[24] Ibid., p.247.
[25] Ibid., p.244.

ABOVE One of the two Panther turrets installed by the Germans to protect the Miramare airfield near Rimini. The turret was knocked out by Lieutenant Collins of 18th NZ Armoured Regiment in the fighting for the Gothic Line in September 1944 and he is pictured next to it with the shell holes visible in the side. (J. Plowman)

BELOW A view of the Il Giogo Pass with Route 6524 winding through the centre. The feature to the left rear is the Monticelli Ridge captured by 91st (US) Infantry Division and front right is Monte Altuzzo captured by 85th (US) Infantry Division. (US National Archives, 321203)

the defences of Green II, but a lack of time and materials meant that no work had been completed. Nevertheless, it was naturally strong and manned by fresh divisions. Moreover, because no work had been completed the Allies were unaware of its existence and assumed that the Germans would fall back to their next prepared position – the Rimini Line. They were wrong. The Germans fought a vigorous rearguard action that provided valuable time for further work to be completed along the Ausa River.

In the middle of September the Germans began to man the Rimini Line in preparation for the next Allied assault, which began soon thereafter. The defences were again softened up by air attacks from the DAF, but bombing could not always neutralize the enemy defences. On 15 September 1944, 3rd Greek Mountain Brigade supported by tanks of 18th New Zealand Armoured Regiment attacked Miramare airfield, near Rimini, which was protected by two emplaced Panther turrets. One of the turrets sited to cover Route 16 (the coast road) had been destroyed by its crew following an earlier engagement with the New Zealanders, but the other remained intact.

On 17 September the Seaforths of Canada supported by a squadron of 145th Regiment RAC put in an attack on San Martino. The attack started well, but soon six of the supporting tanks were knocked out. These it was believed were the victims of the second Panther turret located at the northern end of the airfield. This was engaged by artillery and ground attack aircraft but neither succeeded in silencing the turret. The only alternative was a direct attack by the tanks of 18th NZ Armoured Regiment. But so complete was the turret's command of the terrain that it was decided that the best way of silencing the menace was an attack by a single tank. Covered by smoke the tank, commanded by Lieutenant Collins, advanced to within range of the turret and with its fourth shot knocked it out before escaping under another smoke screen. For his bravery in the battle for Rimini airfield Collins was awarded the Military Cross.

In a little under a month Eighth Army had broken through the three main lines in the Apennines and Leese could rightly claim that his men had smashed 'the powerful Gothic Line defences at very small expense and before the enemy was ready'.[26] Eighth Army now stood on the Plains of Lombardy, but waiting for it was a further series of defensive lines and the autumn rains had come early, which extinguished any lingering hopes of a swift exploitation.

On Fifth Army's front, General Mark Clark planned to make his main thrust through the Apennines towards Bologna. The most direct route, and the weakest point topographically, was along Route 65 through the Futa Pass. However, the Germans had also recognized the significance of this pass and it had been heavily fortified. Moreover, intelligence intercepts suggested that Hitler had ordered Kesselring to concentrate his troops at this strategically important point. In light of this Clark considered his options. The Il Giogio Pass, some 10km east, was a less promising avenue of attack, but it was neither as heavily fortified nor as heavily defended (only one regiment of 4th Fallschirmjäger Division guarded Il Giogio – there were two at the Futa Pass), and it also lay on the boundary between the German Tenth and Fourteenth Armies, and as such was one of the weaker points on the enemy front. A breakthrough

[26] W. Jackson, *The Mediterranean and Middle East, Vol. VI, Victory in the Mediterranean, Part II, June to October 1944* (HMSO, London, 1987)., p.300.

here would outflank the defences of the Futa Pass and open up the possibility of exploitation towards Bologna or Imola.

On 12 September Clark launched his attack. The 91st (US) Infantry Division attacked Il Giogio with 85th (US) Infantry in reserve, while the 34th (US) Infantry Division launched a feint against the Futa Pass. Although undoubtedly less challenging than the Futa Pass, the capture of Il Giogio was nevertheless a daunting prospect. It was dominated by the Monticelli Ridge on the left and Monte Altuzzo on the right. These features had been fortified with the addition of

concrete shelters or positions blasted into the rock that were almost impossible to identify. The main avenues of advance had also been covered with mines and barbed wire.

As the men of 91st (US) Infantry Division made their way up the slopes of the Monticelli Ridge they were engaged by the enemy firing from pillboxes and bunkers. Where possible these were engaged by anti-tank guns, tanks and tank destroyers, while positions out of range or too strong were targeted by heavy-calibre 8in. guns and 240mm howitzers. But in the final reckoning it was down to the infantry to storm the enemy positions using small arms and grenades and, after a sanguinary struggle, the men of 363rd Infantry Regiment managed to secure part of the ridge by 15 September. With the defenders unable to call up reinforcements from the two regiments guarding the Futa Pass, who were themselves under pressure from the holding attack by 34th (US) Infantry Division, the Monticelli Ridge was captured on 18 September. Initially it was believed that 91st (US) Infantry Division would be able to capture this feature and Monte Altuzzo, but the stiff resistance meant that 85th (US) Infantry Division had to be ordered forward to attack the second feature. After further fierce engagements with the tenacious paratroopers the mountain was taken on the same day. The Americans paid a high price for this small section of the Gothic Line – 2,731 casualties – but the important breakthrough had been achieved. The OKW was acutely aware of this fact and Lemelsen, the commander of Fourteenth Army, ordered 4th Fallschirmjäger Division to abandon the Green Line. The formidable defences of the Futa Pass had been outflanked and captured without a fight.

ABOVE One of the two Panther turrets that were positioned to protect the Futa Pass. The presence of these weapons inclined the Americans to attack the less well-defended Il Giogo Pass. (US National Archives, 195989)

LEFT A concrete emplacement that formed part of the Gothic Line defences near the Futa Pass. It would have mounted either a 75mm or 88mm anti-tank gun. The American 91st Division captured this position. (Imperial War Museum, NA 18971)

# Aftermath

In the summer of 1943 the possibility that much if not all of the Italian mainland would escape serious damage seemed bright. Italian forces were continuing to fight in Sicily, but they had little stomach to continue to wage war on the mainland. Mussolini had gone and negotiations for an Italian surrender were under way. However, the negotiations stalled and Hitler, who had previously considered holding a line from Pisa to Rimini, sent his troops further south. It was now clear that the Germans would fight for every inch of ground with the primary aim of keeping the Allies as far away from the heart of the Third Reich as possible, and they would spare little or no regard for the country they were fighting over.

Roads and bridges were demolished to delay the Allies and houses and trees were cleared to provide better fields of fire. But for all that Rome and the other major cultural centres escaped with little or no damage and there were examples where culture triumphed over operational need. In Florence, for example, the Germans destroyed all the bridges over the Arno but following agreement with the Allies, who promised not to use it for military purposes, the Ponte Vecchio was saved.

But equally there were a number of aberrations, the most significant being the Allied bombing of the Benedictine Monastery at Cassino, which it was believed (erroneously as it turned out) was being used by the Germans as an observation post. While it is easy to criticize this action with benefit of hindsight, the attack was ordered with the intention of smashing the Gustav Line and easing the path of the ground forces. Some of the defences were destroyed and more were accounted for in subsequent raids. Others were silenced by artillery fire and by direct fire from tanks.

Indeed during the campaign as a whole many of the defences met a similar fate. Others still were demolished by the crew before they retreated or were simply abandoned. Frequently it was possible for the Allies to ignore them and continue to press the retreating German forces but some simply had to be demolished or, like a number of Panther turrets in the Green Line, lifted and removed to scrap heaps so that engineers could improve old roads, or build

BELOW LEFT With the fighting over, some of the larger defences provided valuable shelter for refugees who had been displaced or whose homes had been destroyed. Here a family takes shelter in an abandoned gun battery near Rimini. (Imperial War Museum, NA18991)

BELOW RIGHT An American soldier inspects the shattered remains of one of the small artillery bunkers (Type 671) installed on the coast near Pisa. These casemates were extensively used along the Atlantic Wall and it would have mounted a 10.5cm gun. (US National Archives, 193029-S)

new ones. This was vital to the success of the Allies, whose lines of communication grew longer the further up the peninsula they advanced. Wherever possible the captured defences were studied by intelligence officers. For much of the campaign Italy was the only front on which the British and Americans were actively fighting and as such this information gave them a valuable insight into German tactics and innovations. It was in Italy that the Allies first came across the German tactic of elastic defence in depth. In terms of equipment the first *MG Panzernest* was encountered here as were dug-in tank turrets used as improvised fixed fortifications. These were later to be found protecting the Normandy beaches and in the West Wall, where emplaced Panther turrets made an

unwelcome reappearance. Detailed reports on these weapons were written and dispatched to the UK and America where they were analysed and the useful information disseminated to front-line units, which proved invaluable in the eventual Allied victory.

After liberation the defences were initially the responsibility of the Allied occupation administration and, later, the newly formed Italian government. Their first priority was the removal of any weapons that were of immediate danger to the civilian population, and as such minefields were cleared by mine-removal teams who suffered many casualties and to whom there is a memorial in Ravenna. Other defences were largely ignored as priority was given to more important tasks like the country's infrastructure, with the reconstruction of bridges, railways and roads that allowed the restoration of the Italian economy. Gradually the defences were erased from the Italian countryside. Many of them were little more than fieldworks and were backfilled with earth. More substantial structures were demolished, removed or sometimes simply covered up. One of the Panther turrets positioned to defend the Poretta pass above Pistoia was demolished by Italian contractors from Leghorn who, having access to no other tools, dynamited the position and collected the valuable scrap metal.

ABOVE American soldiers inspect an *MG Panzernest* that has been installed to cover one of the many beaches. The shield at the front, which was used to protect the aperture when the machine gun was not in use, is clearly visible as are the openings at the side that were used for the axle and for ventilation. The two periscopes at the top can also be seen. (US National Archives, 192342)

LEFT Engineers pass through dragon's teeth with mines they have removed from a site that is to be an airfield. Many died undertaking this dangerous but important task. (Imperial War Museum, NA21251)

57

# The sites today

After the war the vast majority of German defences built in Italy were demolished, removed or simply filled in. But in spite of this a number of the defences did survive. Dragon's teeth can still be seen on the coast near Ravenna along with a number of bunkers on the Lido di Venezia, a strip of land that separates the Venetian Lagoon from the Adriatic Sea. It is also possible to find some evidence of the defences around the Futa Pass, although no attempt has been made to preserve the remains or make them accessible to visitors.

One word of warning though, although visiting the battlefields of Italy is to be thoroughly recommended, visitors should respect private property and should be aware of the dangers of munitions that may still be live. In no circumstances should items be picked up and certainly should not be removed. Provided visitors follow this rule they should have a safe and enjoyable stay.

## Museums and other sites of interest

### Cassino

Somewhat surprisingly considering the profile of the battle there is no major museum or exhibition devoted to the battle of Monte Cassino. The Cassino War Museum is a small privately run affair located on the outskirts of the town and, although poorly signposted, is worth a visit.

But if the lack of an officially sponsored museum is disappointing the fully restored Benedictine Monastery that dominates the town is not. This was completely destroyed by Allied bombers during the fighting for Cassino, but after the war was rebuilt. The work took more than a decade and although there are no military exhibits it is well worth a visit. Visitors should dress appropriately to respect the fact that this is a place of worship.

In the shadow of the Monastery is the Polish War Cemetery, which is the resting place of almost 1,000 soldiers of Anders' II Polish Corps. Also worth a visit is the Polish Memorial created from a Sherman tank at Albaneta Farm.

Nearly 2km south-west of the town is the Cassino War Cemetery. This is the largest Commonwealth war cemetery in Italy and, as with all the cemeteries managed by the Commonwealth War Graves Commission, it is beautifully maintained. The rows of pristine headstones are particularly poignant lying as they do in the shadow of the Monastery where so many of these men fell. More than 4,000 Allied servicemen are buried in the cemetery with a further 4,000 casualties who have no known grave commemorated by the Cassino Memorial.

A short drive by car brings visitors to the Minturno Cemetery, where 2,000 more Allied servicemen who perished in the fighting for the Gustav Line are buried.

North of Cassino at Caira is the German war cemetery where more than 20,000 soldiers who fell fighting in the Italian campaign are commemorated. It is also well maintained but, like so many German cemeteries, is very low key.

### Anzio

A little further north is Anzio where the Allies landed in January 1944 – the western anchor of the Caesar Line was on the coast just north of the beachhead. It is feasible to visit the town from Cassino or if visitors are based in Rome. Again there is little or nothing left

BELOW As an alternative to dragon's teeth, barbed wire was sometimes laced between screw pickets in a slightly more haphazard, but equally effective, manner. Good examples of this were the entanglements that protected the beaches near Ravenna at the rear of the Gothic Line. (Imperial War Museum, NA20889)

of the defences, but visitors can visit the Anzio Beachhead Museum, which was opened in 1994 to commemorate the 50th anniversary of the Anzio landings. It is located in the Villa Adele, which is situated in the centre of the town and is easily reached from the railway station. The museum is small but has many interesting exhibits including a short film about the landings. The museum has limited opening times, but entrance is free. Check details on the Internet site before visiting – http://www.sbarcodianzio.it/.

ABOVE Some of the dragon's teeth that were constructed on the Adriatic coast to prevent an Allied landing. These were positioned to the south of Ravenna. Barbed wire secured to stakes rammed into the ground provided passive anti-infantry protection. (Imperial War Museum, NA20024)

There are also two Commonwealth cemeteries in the locality. Anzio War Cemetery lies 1km north of Anzio town and is the resting place of more than 1,000 Allied servicemen. Beach Head Cemetery, which is located a little further north, is much larger and contains over 2,000 burials.

The Sicily–Rome American Cemetery and Memorial is also near to Anzio at the north edge of the town of Nettuno. The cemetery site covers more than 28ha and is the resting place of almost 8,000 American military dead who lost their lives in Sicily and during the landings on the mainland including Anzio.

### Gothic Line
There are a number of small privately run museums that are devoted to the battle for the Gothic Line. The Museo Storico della Linea Gotica, or Gothic Line Museum, is located at Casinina near Auditore, not far from Pesaro. The museum has a number of galleries that hold some 3,000 exhibits. It is open daily from 9am until 7pm but is closed at lunchtime. The Museo di Monte Gridolfo is only a short distance away and is situated in Montegridolfo castle (Email: montegridolfo@provincia.rimini.it). It includes examples of weapons, and personal equipment mostly donated by local inhabitants. In addition, the museum has a collection of newspapers and magazines from the period and it is also possible to watch films dating from World War II.

Again there are a number of cemeteries that are well worth visiting in and around the Gothic Line. The Coriano Ridge War Cemetery is located 3km west of Riccione on the Adriatic coast. Although not forming part of the Gothic Line proper the Coriano Ridge was an important feature in the way of the Allied advance in the Adriatic sector in the autumn of 1944. It fell to the Allies in the middle of September but the price was high and some 2,000 servicemen, most of whom fell in this action, are commemorated here. West of Pesaro is the Montecchio war cemetery. This stands on ground above the old anti-tank ditch and is the final resting place of some 600 servicemen, mostly Canadians. A further 1,200 Allied servicemen who fell in the battle for the Gothic Line are buried in the Gradara War Cemetery, which is situated between Pesaro and Riccione.

BELOW An Allied soldier emerges through the embrasure of a gun position that was hewn in the side of a mountain. The position covered the road that ran down the Serchio Valley near Gallicano. The opening was camouflaged with stone cladding. (Imperial War Museum, NA21202)

Further west is the Florence American Cemetery and Memorial. This is located about 12km south of Florence and is served by a regular bus service. The site covers 28ha and is where more than a third of the American forces in Italy are buried – over 4,000 – with most having been killed in the advance north of Rome.

# Getting there
There are regular flights from London Heathrow and Gatwick to Rome and to Pisa, as well as to Bologna (using an alliance carrier) from Gatwick. The budget airlines also operate low-cost flights from the UK to various airports in Italy, although these often tend to be some distance from city centres. The principal Italian carrier, Alitalia, also operates flights from

ABOVE An Italian Cannone de 76/40. This was a dual-purpose AA/coastal defence gun of World War I origin that has been installed in a fieldwork in the Gothic Line. The shells are stored in a niche at the front. In the background British troops receive a briefing. (Imperial War Museum, NA 19092)

Heathrow and other regional airports to Ancona, Bologna, Florence, Pisa, Rimini and Rome, which are all ideally suited for visiting the main battlefields. From the United States the main national airlines all offer direct flights to Italy.

From the UK it is possible to travel to Italy by rail. Eurostar services travel daily to Paris and Brussels from where onward connections to Italy can be organized. There is a good train network in Italy (visit the national rail website at http://www.trenitalia.it/) but, with the exception of Cassino, it is difficult to reach the main battlefields from the stations without a car.

It is also possible to drive from the UK. Cross-channel ferries or Eurotunnel take cars to the Continent and there are a number of good routes that take you through the Swiss or Austrian Alps to Italy. This mode of transport will take you through the defensive lines in reverse order with the Voralpenstellung, Gothic Line first and much further south the Hitler and Gustav lines. An alternative is to transport the car by train, but this can be expensive.

## Getting around

Once in Italy it is relatively easy to travel around. There is a good rail and bus service, but, as has been mentioned, to reach the sites of interest it is generally necessary to have a car. This can be privately owned or a hire car, which is easy to organize at the major airports and rail stations.

Visiting Monte Cassino from Rome is straightforward by car. Leaving the airport you pick up the Rome ring road and head for the A1 Autostrada (motorway) south, which takes you along the Liri Valley where you take the exit for Cassino. The A1 is a toll road, but is reasonably priced and has along its route a number of service stations which offer good-quality reasonably priced food and drink. You can also take the old Route 6 from Rome south, which is the route that the Allies took, but it will take you longer. Anzio is also driveable from Rome and it is possible to take a day trip for visitors based in Cassino.

The eastern extension of the Gothic Line where the British and Commonwealth forces were primarily engaged are best reached from Rimini or Ancona airports. The American sector is more straightforward from Bologna or Florence. These have the added attraction of offering the visitor the chance to visit two of the great cultural centres in Italy.

## Staying there

Italy is a popular holiday destination and there are numerous hotels, rental accommodation and camp sites and the choice will very much depend on which battlefields the visitor intends on visiting and the type of accommodation preferred.

A number of useful Internet sites are available to visitors to help them decide the best alternative. The Italian embassy web site (http://www.embitaly.org.uk/) has a number of useful links besides a wealth of other valuable information for visitors, as does the Italian tourist information office (http://www.italiantourism.com/) for American visitors.

One specific hotel worthy of mention is the Hotel La Place, which is a three-star hotel situated in Cassino town and only a short distance from Castle Hill and the Monastery itself. It also has the added attraction of housing a number of artefacts from the battle. Further details can be found at http://www.cassinohotel.it/

Heading further north, the Adriatic coast around Rimini has many beaches and is well served by all types of accommodation that are within easy striking distance of the main Gothic Line defences on the east coast.

# German defensive lines in Italy

A Line – followed Biferno River (*see* Viktor Line)
A1 Line – followed Volturno River (*see* Viktor Line)
Adelheid Line
Adige Line (*see* Venetian Line)
Albert Line
Alpenfestung (Alpine Fortress)
Anna Line
Anton Line
Augsberger Line
B Line (*see* Bernhardt Line)
Barbara Line
Bernhardt Line (*or* B Line *or* Rheinhardt/Reinhard
    Line)
Blue Line (*see* Voralpenstellung)
Caesar Line
Campagna Switch Line
Dora Line – extension to the Hitler Line
Dora Line – rallying position north of Rome
Line E
Erika Line
Etna Line (*or* Old Hube Line *or* San Fratello Line)
Foro Line
Frieda Line (*see* Albert Line)
Genghis Khan Line (*or* Reno Line)
Georg Line
Gothic Line (renamed Green Line in June 1944)
Green Line I (*or* Gothic Line)
Green Line II (*or* Gothic Line)
Gudrun Position
Gustav Line
Hauptkampflinie
Heinrich Line
Hitler Line (*or* Senger Line)
Irmgard Line
Laura Line

Lilo Line
Lydia Line
Mädchen Line
Massa Line
Mt. S Michele Line
New Hube Line
O Line
Old Hube (*see* Etna Line)
Olga Line
Orange Line
Paula Line – delaying position in front of Florence
Paula Line – delaying position in front of the
    Voralpenstellung
Pisa-Rimini Line (*see* Gothic/Green Line)
Red Line (forward position of Gothic/Green Line)
Red Line (*see* Venetian Line)
Reno Line (*see* Genghis Khan Line)
Rheinhardt/Reinhard Line (*see* Bernhardt Line)
Rimini Line
San Fratello Line (*see* Etna Line)
Sangro/Advanced Sangro Line (*or* Siegfried Line)
Senger Line (*see* Hitler Line)
Siegfried Line (*see* Sangro Line)
Trasimene Line (*see* Albert Line)
Valmontone Line (Allied name for part of Caesar
    Line)
Venetian Line (*or* Adige Line)
Viktor Line (*or* Line A / A1)
Voralpenstellung (Forward Alpine Position *or* Blue
    Line)
Vorfeld Line
Water Line – to protect against a possible landing on
    the Venice–Trieste coast
Winter Line (Allied term for Bernhardt/Gustav/Hitler
    Line)

# Bibliography and further reading

## Primary sources

Bundesarchiv, Freiburg
Canadian National Archives, Ottawa
Imperial War Museum, London
National Archives, London

## Secondary sources

Anonymous, *Bildheft Neuzeitlicher Stellungbau*, Merkblatt 57/5,15 September 1942. Reprinted as *German Fieldworks of World War II* (Bellona Publications Limited: Bracknell, 1969)

Fleischer, W., *Feldbefestigungen des deutschen Heeres 1939–1945* (Podzun-Pallas: Wölersheim-Berstadt, 1998)

Kaufmann J. E., and Kaufmann, H. W., *Fortress Third Reich – German Fortifications and Defence Systems in World War II* (Greenhill Books: London, 2003)

Rottman, G. L., *Fortress 23: German Field Fortifications 1939–45* (Osprey Publishing: Oxford, 2004)

### Articles

Clerici C., and Vajna de Pava, E., 'Coastal Defences of Genoa During the Second World War', *Fort*, Vol. 23 (1995), p.111–126

Guglielmi, D. 'Linee fortificate tedesche in Italia 1943–1945', *Storia & Battaglie* p.21–32

## Further reading

D'Este, C., *Bitter Victory: The Battle for Sicily July–August 1943* (Collins: London, 1988)

Ellis, J., *Cassino. The Hollow Victory: The Battle For Rome January–June 1944* (Andre Deutsch, London, 1984)

Fisher, E., *Cassino to the Alps* (Center for Military History: Washington, 1977)

Garland A., and McGaw Smyth, H., *Sicily and the Surrender of Italy* (Center of Military History: Washington, 1986)

Jackson, W., *The Battle for Italy* (Harper and Row: New York, 1967)

Jackson, W., *The Battle for Rome* (Batsford: London, 1969)

Jackson, W., *The Mediterranean and Middle East, Vol. VI, Victory in the Mediterranean, Part II, June to October 1944* (HMSO: London, 1987)

Jackson, W., *The Mediterranean and Middle East, Vol. VI, Victory in the Mediterranean, Part III, November 1944 to May 1945* (HMSO: London, 1988)

Molony, C., *The Mediterranean and Middle East, Vol. V, The Campaign in Sicily and the Campaign in Italy, 3rd September to 31st March 1944* (HMSO: London, 1973)

Molony, C., *The Mediterranean and Middle East, Vol. VI, Victory in the Mediterranean, Part I, 1st April to 4th June 1944* (HMSO: London, 1986)

Orgill, D., *The Gothic Line, The Autumn Campaign in Italy, 1944* (Pan Books Ltd: London, 1967)

Starr, C., *From Salerno to the Alps: a History of the Fifth Army 1943–1945* (Infantry Journal Press: Washington, 1948)

# Glossary

**AOK:** See *Armee Oberkommando*

**Armee Oberkommando:** Army HQ Staff

**Bunker:** General term for any kind of strengthened fighting post. Originally referred to a shelter or a store.

**Casemate:** Originally a bombproof chamber built for cannon or to provide barrack accommodation. The German military tended to use the term in respect of their flanking installations.

**Crab:** *MG Panzernest*

**DAF:** Desert Air Force

**Embrasure:** An opening in a bunker through which a gun may be fired.

**Fallschirmjäger:** German paratrooper

**Feldmaßig:** field installations being a temporary fieldworks rather than permanent fortifications

**Fest Pi Kdr:** See *Festungspionierkommandeur*

**Fest Pi Stab:** See *Festungspionierstab*

**Festungspionierkommandeur:** Fortification engineer commander

**Festungspionierstab:** Fortification engineer staff

**Festung:** fortress

**Festungspanzerdrehturm:** Fortification armoured rotating turret

**Fieldwork:** A non-permanent fortification, generally constructed from earth and timber, although sometimes reinforced with concrete

**Flak:** See *Flugzeugabwehrkanone.*

**Flugzeugabwehrkanone (Flak):** Anti-aircraft gun

**F Pz DT:** See *Festungspanzerdrehturm*

**Heeresgruppe:** Army group

**Höckerhindernis:** 'Dragon's teeth'. Rows of linked concrete obstacles designed to stop tanks

**Kampfwagenkanone (Kwk):** Tank gun

**Kwk:** See *Kampfwagenkanone*

**Luftwaffe:** German Air Force

**Nebelwerfer:** German five- or six-barrelled rocket launcher

**Organization Todt (OT):** Paramilitary organisation employed in the construction of major state and party building programmes

**Ostwallturm:** Specially designed Panther turret

**OT:** See Organization Todt

**Pak:** See *Panzerabwehrkanone*

**Pantherturm Kompanie:** Panther turret company

**Panzerabwehrgraben:** anti-tank trap

**Panzerabwehrkanone (Pak):** Anti-tank gun

**Panzerfaust:** German hand held anti-tank weapon

**Pillbox:** British term coined in World War I to describe concrete machine-gun shelters

**Pioneer (Pionier):** German term for engineers

**RAC:** Royal Armoured Corps

**Regelbau:** standard fortification design

**RTR:** Royal Tank Regiment

**S-Mine:** German anti-personnel mine

**Stellung:** Position or line

**Tellermine:** German anti-tank mine

**Tobruk:** Small concrete structure with ring shaped opening at the top primarily designed to accommodate a machine gun

**Wehrmacht:** German Armed Forces

# Index